IP-889

The Yellow Pages

for Students & Teachers

from
the kids' stuff people

ACKNOWLEDGEMENTS

Special acknowledgement is gratefully accorded

   . . . to Eleanor L. Dunn, Robert J. Shaffer and Mary Ann Pangle for researching and organizing many of the lists found in the Teacher's Yellow Pages section,

   . . . and to Elaine Raphael, editor, critic and contributor, my appreciation is boundless.

Library of Congress Catalog Card Number: 79-93126
ISBN 0-913916-88-9

READING

TABLE OF CONTENTS

SHORT A WORDS

add	chance	grab	pad	slap
after	clam	grand	pal	slat
ant	clamp	grant	pan	snag
ask	clasp	grass	pant	snap
at	class	had	pass	span
ax	crack	ham	past	splash
back	cramp	hand	pat	stab
bad	crash	handle	plan	stack
bag	dad	hat	plant	stamp
bat	dam	jab	quack	tab
bath	damp	jam	rack	tacks
black	dance	lab	raft	tag
bland	dash	lamb	rag	tan
brand	drab	lamp	ram	task
brass	fact	land	ran	than
cab	fan	last	rang	that
camp	fat	mad	rap	track
can	flag	man	rat	trap
candle	flat	map	sack	trash
cap	gal	mask	sad	vamp
cash	gap	master	sand	van
cast	gas	match	sang	vast
cat	glance	nag	scab	wax
catch	glass	nap	scrap	yam
champ	gnat	pack	slab	

SHORT E WORDS

beck	dwell	ledge	quench	them
bed	edge	left	red	then
beg	egg	leg	rent	vent
bell	elbow	less	rest	vest
bench	ever	let	scent	vet
bend	fed	level	sell	vex
bent	fell	men	send	web
best	fence	mend	sent	wed
bet	fetch	mess	shed	wedge
bled	fleck	met	shell	well
blend	fled	neck	shred	went
bless	flesh	nest	sled	wept
bred	fresh	net	sledge	west
cell	gem	never	slept	wet
cent	get	next	smell	when
center	hedge	pebble	sped	wreck
chest	helmet	peck	spell	wrench
clef	help	peg	spend	yell
crest	hem	pen	spent	yelp
deck	hen	pep	stress	yes
dell	jelly	pest	swept	yet
dense	jest	pet	tell	zest
dent	jet	pledge	ten	
desk	kept	press	tent	
dress	led	quell	test	

SHORT I WORDS

bib	ill	pinch	strip
bid	in	pit	swim
big	inch	rib	thin
bill	jig	rid	thing
bin	kick	rift	this
brick	kid	rig	tickle
bridge	king	rill	till
chick	kiss	rim	tin
chin	knit	rip	tip
dig	lid	risk	twin
dill	lift	ship	twist
dim	limb	shrill	vim
dip	lint	sick	vision
dish	lip	sift	whim
fib	list	silk	whip
fig	lit	simmer	whiskers
fill	milk	sin	whistle
film	miss	sip	wick
fish	mist	sister	wiff
fist	mister	sit	wig
fix	mitt	six	will
grin	nibble	skill	win
grip	nick	slit	wing
hid	nil	spill	wit
hill	nip	split	with
him	pick	stick	wrist
hint	picnic	still	yip
his	pig	sting	zip
hit	pin	stitch	

SHORT O WORDS

block	cost	hock	monster	shod
bog	cot	hog	mop	shop
bomb	crock	hop	moss	shot
bond	crop	hot	moth	slob
boss	cross	job	nod	slop
bottle	dock	jot	not	slosh
box	dodge	knob	on	slot
broth	dog	knock	ox	smock
chop	doll	knot	plod	smog
clock	dollar	lock	plop	snob
clod	dot	lodge	plot	sob
clog	drop	loft	pocket	sock
clop	flop	log	pod	song
closet	fog	lollipop	pond	spot
cloth	fond	lop	pop	stock
cob	forgot	loss	pot	stop
cock	fox	lost	rob	top
cod	frost	lot	rock	toss
cog	gloss	mob	rod	
common	gob	mock	rot	
con	got	mod	rotten	
cop	hobble	mom	shock	

SHORT U WORDS

bluff
blunt
blush
brunch
buck
bud
buff
bug
bum
bump
bun
bunch
bundle
bunt
bus
but
buzz
clump
clutch
crumb
crunch
crust
cub
cuff
cull
cup
cut
drudge
drug
drum
duck
dug
dull
dumb
dump
dusk
dust
fluff
flung
flush
fluster
fudge
fun
fund
fuss

fuzz
glum
glut
grub
grudge
gruff
grump
gull
gum
gun
gush
gut
gutter
hub
huff
hug
hull
hum
humble
hump
hunch
hung
hunt
husk
hut
jug
jump
just
jut
luck
lug
lull
lump
lunch
lung
muck
mud
mug
mull
munch
mush
must
null
nut
pluck

plum
plunge
plus
pulp
pump
punch
pup
rub
ruffle
rug
rum
run
rung
rush
rust
rut
skull
skunk
slug
slum
slump
sprung
struck
stun
stunt
sun
sung
sunk
swung
truck
trunk
trust
tub
tuck
tug
tusk
ugly
umbrella
uncle
under
unjust
until
up
us

LONG A WORDS (SILENT E)

ace	cave	glade	mistake	shape
agape	chase	glaze	name	skate
age	crate	grace	nape	slate
ale	crave	grade	pace	slave
amaze	date	grape	page	snake
ape	daze	grate	pave	space
ate	deface	grave	place	spade
babe	disgrace	graze	plane	stage
bale	drake	hale	plate	stake
bake	drape	hate	quake	stale
base	engage	haze	race	state
bathe	enrage	jade	rage	stave
blame	evade	knave	rake	take
blaze	exhale	lace	rape	tale
behave	face	lake	rate	tame
brace	fade	lame	rave	tape
brake	fake	lane	sage	thane
brave	fame	late	sake	trace
cage	fate	lathe	sale	trade
cake	flake	mace	same	vale
came	flame	made	sane	vane
cane	gale	make	save	wade
cape	game	male	scrape	wage
case	gate	mane	shade	
	gave	mate	shake	
	gaze	maze	shame	

LONG I WORDS (SILENT E)

abide	grime	price	strive
advice	gripe	prime	swipe
advise	hive	prize	thrice
arrive	ice	rice	thrive
aside	ire	rife	tile
beside	kite	rile	time
bide	knife	ripe	tire
bile	lice	rise	tribe
bite	life	rite	tripe
bribe	lime	scribe	twice
bride	line	shine	vice
brine	live	shrine	vile
chide	mice	shire	vine
chime	mile	sire	vise
chive	mime	size	while
cite	mine	slice	whine
crime	mire	slime	white
fife	mite	smile	wide
file	nice	spice	wife
fine	nine	splice	wine
fire	pile	stile	wipe
five	pine	strife	wire
glide	pipe	stripe	wise

LONG O WORDS (SILENT E)

bode	grope	rode
bone	hole	rope
broke	home	rose
choke	hone	rote
chose	hope	rove
chrome	hose	scope
clone	hove	slope
close	joke	smoke
clothe	lobe	smote
clove	lone	sole
coke	lope	stoke
cone	mode	stole
cope	mole	stone
cove	mope	stove
crone	node	strobe
dole	nose	strode
dome	note	stroke
dope	phone	those
dose	poke	throne
dote	pole	tone
doze	pope	tote
drone	pose	vote
drove	probe	woke
froze	prone	yoke
globe	quote	zone
	robe	

LONG U WORDS (SILENT E)

brute	dude	huge	prude	spruce
butte	duke	jute	prune	tube
chute	dune	mule	puke	tune
crude	dupe	mute	pure	yule
cube	flute	nude	rule	
cute	fume		ruse	

FINAL Y

Long E

alley	factory	hockey	lucky	quickly
army	fairy	honey	memory	rocky
baby	family	hungry	money	stingy
bunny	fancy	hurry	mystery	study
bury	funny	ivory	naughty	surgery
busy	furry	ivy	navy	taffy
canary	fury	jockey	nursery	tiny
city	glory	journey	party	twenty
country	grocery	jury	penny	ugly
county	happy	lady	plenty	very
drowsy	hardy	lazy	pony	weary
easy	heavy	liberty	poppy	zany

Long I

buy
by
cry
dry
fly
fry
my
ply
pry
shy
sky
sly
spry
spy
sty
try
why
wry

6

VOWEL DIGRAPHS (FIRST VOWEL LONG)

-AI- (long a)

aid	drain	lain	quail	tail
aide	fail	maid	quaint	taint
ail	fain	mail	raid	trail
aim	faint	maim	rail	train
bail	faith	main	rain	trait
bait	flail	maize	raise	twain
braid	frail	nail	sail	vain
brain	gain	paid	saint	waif
braise	gaily	pail	slain	wail
chain	gait	pain	snail	wain
chaise	grain	paint	staid	waist
claim	hail	plain	stain	wait
daily	jail	plait	strain	waive
dainty	laid	praise	strait	

-AY- (long a)

bay	dray	hay	pay	spray
bray	flay	jay	play	splay
clay	fray	lay	ray	stay
crayon	gay	may	say	stray
day	gray	nay	slay	tray
				way

-EA- (long e)

beach	crease	heal	peach	seat
bead	deal	heap	peak	sneak
beak	dean	heat	peal	speak
beam	decease	heave	peat	squeak
bean	decrease	knead	plea	squeal
beast	disease	lead	plead	steal
beat	dream	leaf	please	steam
bleach	each	leak	pleat	streak
bleak	eagle	lean	preach	tea
bleat	ease	leap	reach	teach
breach	east	least	read	teak
cease	eat	leave	real	team
cheap	feast	meal	ream	treat
clean	feat	mean	reap	tweak
cleat	freak	meat	scream	veal
cleave	gleam	neat	sea	weak
creak	glean	pea	seal	yeast
cream	grease	peace	seam	zeal

7

VOWEL DIGRAPHS (FIRST VOWEL LONG)

-EE- (long e)

bee	feed	keen	screen	
beech	feel	knee	seed	steel
beep	feet	lee	seep	steep
between	flee	leech	seek	steeple
bleed	fleece	leek	seem	street
breech	fleet	meek	seen	teem
breed	free	meet	sheen	teeth
breeze	freed	need	sheep	thee
cheek	freeze	peek	sheet	three
cheese	geese	peel	sleep	tree
creed	glee	peep	sleet	tweed
creek	greed	peeve	sleeve	weed
creep	green	preen	sneeze	weep
deed	greet	queen	speech	wheel
deep	heed	reed	speed	wheeze
deem	heel	reek	spleen	
eel	jeep	reel	spree	
fee	keel	screech	squeeze	

-OA- (long o)

afloat	croak	load	oaken	shoat
bloat	float	loaf	oat	soak
boast	foal	loafer	oath	soap
boat	foam	loam	poach	throat
broach	gloaming	loan	poacher	toad
cloak	gloat	loath	roach	toast
coach	goad	loathe	road	toaster
coal	goal	loaves	roam	whoa
coast	goat	moan	roan	
coaster	groan	moat	roast	
coat	groat	oaf	roaster	
coax	hoax	oak	shoal	

8

VOWEL DIGRAPHS

-OO- (boot)

bloom	hoot	scoop
boom	loom	shoot
boot	loop	sloop
boost	loose	spoof
booster	loot	spool
brood	mood	spoon
cool	moose	smooth
coop	noon	snooze
doom	noose	stool
drool	pool	stoop
droop	proof	swoop
food	roof	too
fool	room	toot
gloom	roost	tooth
goose	rooster	troop
groom	root	whoop
hoop	school	zoo

-OO- (book)

book	good	poor
boor	hood	rook
brook	hoof	shook
cook	hook	soot
cookies	look	stood
crook	moor	took
foot	nook	wool

-UE

acrue	due	gruel
blue	duel	hue
clue	ensue	rue
cruel	fuel	sue
cue	glue	true

DIPHTHONGS

-AU-

applause
auction
audience
audit
audition
aught
augment
august
auk
austere
authentic
author
auto
autograph
autumn
bauble
because
caucus
caught
caulk

cause
caustic
caution
clause
daub
daughter
daunt
exaust
fault
faun
flaunt
fraud
fraught
gaudy
gaunt
gauze
haughty
haul
haunch
haunt

jaunt
laud
launch
launder
laundry
laurel
maul
naughty
nausea
pauper
paunch
pause
sauce
saunter
taught
taunt
taut
vault

-AW-

awe
awesome
awning
bawl
brawl
brawn
caw
claw
craw
crawl
dawn
draw
drawl
drawn
fawn
flaw
gnaw
hawk
hawthorn
jaw
law

lawn
lawyer
mohawk
paw
pawl
pawn
prawn
raw
saw
scrawl
shawl
slaw
spawn
sprawl
squaw
straw
thaw
trawl
withdraw
yawn

-EW-

anew
askew
bedew
blew
brew
chew
clew
crew

dew
drew
flew
grew
hew
jewel
knew
lewd

mew
new
newt
pew
renew
review
shrew
skew

slew
spew
stew
strew
threw
view
yew

-OI-

adjoin
anoint
appoint
asteroid
avoid
boil
broil
choice
coil
coin
conjoint
counterpoint

despoil
devoid
disappoint
disjointed
embroil
enjoin
foil
foist
hoist
join
joint
joist

loin
moil
moist
noise
oil
ointment
purloin
point
poise
quoin
quoit
recoil

rejoice
rejoin
roil
soil
spoil
subjoin
toil
turmoil
voice
void

DIPHTHONGS

-OU-

abound
about
account
aground
aloud
amount
announce
astound
avouch
becloud
blouse
bough
bounce
bound
bout
cloud
clout
compound
confound
couch
count
crouch
denounce

devour
devout
discount
doubt
douse
enshroud
expound
flounce
flounder
flour
flout
foul
found
fount
gout
grouch
ground
grouse
grout
hound
house
impound
joust

loud
louse
lout
mound
mouse
mouth
noun
ouch
ounce
our
out
paramount
pouch
pound
pout
profound
pronounce
rebound
remount
renounce
resound
round
route

scour
scout
shout
shroud
slouch
sound
sour
south
spout
sprout
stout
surmount
surround
thou
tout
trounce
trout
vouch
without
wound

-OW-

allow
bow
bower
brow
brown
chow
chowder
clown
cow
cower
cowl
crowd
crown
down
drown
endow
flower
fowl
frown
glower
gown
growl

how
howitzer
howl
jowl
now
owl
plow
pow
powder
power
prow
prowl
renown
row
scow
shower
sow
town
vow
wow
yowl

-OY-

annoy
boy
cloy
convoy
coy
decoy
deploy
destroy
employ
enjoy
gargoyle
joy
loyal
ploy
royal
toy
troy

11

R CONTROLLED WORDS

-AR-

afar	carnation	far	march	shark
arc	carp	farm	mark	sharp
are	carpet	gar	market	smart
ark	cart	garb	mart	spar
arm	carton	garment	par	spark
art	cartoon	guard	parcel	star
bar	carve	hard	parch	starch
barb	char	hark	pardon	stark
bard	charcoal	harm	park	start
bargain	charge	harmony	part	tar
barge	charm	harp	partridge	tart
bark	chart	jar	party	tsar
barn	dark	lard	radar	yard
car	darn	large	sardine	yarn
card	dart	lark	scar	
cardinal	depart	mar	scarf	

-ER-

after	jerk	perfect	pert	stern
berth	jersey	perform	pertinent	summer
clerk	merchant	perfume	reverse	supper
cover	mercury	perhaps	rubber	swerve
enter	mercy	perjury	runner	teacher
farmer	mermaid	perk	serf	term
fern	miserable	permanent	serge	terminal
germ	nerve	permission	sermon	termite
hammer	offer	permit	serpent	tern
her	percale	perplex	servant	terrain
herb	percent	persist	serve	verse
herd	perception	person	service	winter
hermit	perch	perspire	silver	wonder
hunter	percussion	persuade	sitter	

-IR-

affirm	dirt	girt	skirt	thirty
birch	fir	girth	smirch	thirst
bird	firm	irk	smirk	twirl
birth	first	mirth	squirrel	whir
chirp	firth	quirk	squirt	whirl
circle	flirt	shirk	stir	
circus	gird	shirt	swirl	
dirk	girl	sir	third	

R CONTROLLED WORDS

-OR-

abhor	for	normal	sport
abort	ford	north	store
absorb	forge	or	stork
accord	fork	orb	storm
adorn	form	porch	sword
assort	forth	pork	thorn
bore	glory	port	torch
born	gorge	record	tore
chord	horn	report	torn
chore	horse	score	tornado
consort	ignore	scorn	tort
cord	important	shore	worn
core	lord	short	
cork	lorn	snore	
corn	morn	sore	
distort	nor	sort	

-UR-

blur	cursive	purge	surround
blurt	curt	purl	surtax
burden	curtain	purple	survey
burdock	curtsy	purpose	survive
burg	curve	purr	turban
burglar	fur	purse	turbine
burlap	furl	return	turbulent
burn	furnish	slur	turf
burnt	furniture	spur	turkey
burr	furrow	spurn	turmoil
burro	further	spurt	turn
burrow	hurdle	surf	turnip
burst	hurl	surface	turpentine
church	hurricane	surge	turquoise
churn	hurry	surgeon	turret
cur	hurt	surmise	turtle
curb	hurtle	surname	urban
curd	lurch	surpass	urchin
curfew	lurk	surplus	urge
curl	nurse	surprise	urgent
current	nursery	surrender	urn
curse	nurture	surrey	

CONSONANT BLENDS

BL-

blab	blaze	blimp	blob	blotter
black	blazer	blind	block	blouse
bladder	bleach	blinder	blockade	blow
blade	bleacher	blindfold	bloke	blower
blame	bleak	blink	blond	blubber
blanch	bleary	blintz	blood	blue
bland	bleat	blip	bloodhound	blueprint
blank	bleed	bliss	bloodshed	bluff
blanket	blemish	blister	bloody	blunder
blare	blend	blithe	bloom	blunt
blarney	blender	blithering	blooper	blur
blast	bless	blitz	blossom	blurb
blat	blew	blizzard	blot	blurt
blatant	blight	bloat	blotch	blush

BR-

brace	brat	breeze	brink	brood
bracelet	brave	brevity	brisk	brook
bracken	brawl	brew	bristle	broom
bracket	brawn	briar	britches	broth
brad	bray	bribe	brittle	brother
brag	brazen	brick	broach	brought
braid	brazier	bride	broad	brow
braille	breach	bridge	brocade	brown
brain	breadth	bridle	broccoli	brownie
braise	break	brief	brochure	browse
brake	breakfast	brier	brogue	bruin
bramble	breast	brig	broil	bruise
bran	breath	brigade	broiler	brunch
branch	breathe	brigand	broke	brunt
brand	bred	bright	broken	brush
brandish	breech	brilliant	broker	brusque
brandy	breeches	brim	bronco	brutal
brash	breed	brine	bronze	brute

CL-

clack	clarinet	clef	clinic	clot
clad	clarity	cleft	clink	cloth
claim	clash	clemency	clip	clothe
clam	clasp	clench	clipper	clothes
clamber	class	clergy	clique	cloud
clammy	classic	clerical	cloak	clout
clamor	classify	clerk	clobber	clove
clamp	clatter	clever	clock	clover
clan	clause	click	clod	clown
clang	claw	client	clog	club
clank	clay	cliff	cloister	cluck
clap	clean	climate	clone	clue
clapboard	cleanser	climax	clop	clump
clapper	clear	climb	close	clumsy
claptrap	cleat	clinch	closet	cluster
clarify	cleave	cling	closure	clutch

CONSONANT BLENDS

CR-

crab	cravat	creepy	crisp	crow
crack	crave	cremate	critic	crowd
cracker	craw	crepe	critical	crown
crackle	crawl	crept	criticize	crucial
cradle	crayfish	crescent	critter	crucify
craft	crayon	cress	croak	crud
crafty	craze	crest	crochet	crude
crag	crazy	crevasse	crock	cruel
cram	creak	crevice	crocodile	cruet
cramp	cream	crew	crocus	cruise
cranberry	crease	crib	crone	crumb
crane	create	crick	crony	crumble
cranial	creation	cricket	crook	crumpet
crank	creator	crier	crooked	crumple
cranky	creature	crime	croon	crunch
cranny	credit	crimp	crop	crusade
crappie	creed	crimson	croquet	crutch
crash	creek	cringe	cross	crux
crass	creel	crinkle	crouch	cry
crate	creep	cripple	croup	crypt

DR-

drab	drape	dregs	drivel	drowsy
dracma	drastic	drench	driver	drub
draft	drat	dress	drizzle	drudge
draftsman	draw	dresser	droll	drug
drafty	drawer	dressing	dromedary	druid
drag	drawl	drew	drone	drum
dragon	drawn	dribble	drool	drunk
drain	dray	drier	droop	dry
drake	dread	drift	dropper	dryad
dram	dream	drill	drought	dryly
drama	dreamer	drink	drove	
dramatic	dreary	drip	drown	
drank	dredge	drive	drowse	

FL-

flabbergast	flask	flew	floe	flown
flabby	flat	flex	flog	fluctuate
flag	flatten	flexible	flood	flue
flagon	flatter	flick	floor	fluent
flagrant	flaunt	flier	floozy	fluff
flail	flavor	flight	flop	fluid
flair	flaw	flimsy	floral	fluke
flake	flax	flinch	florist	flume
flame	flay	fling	floss	flunk
flamingo	flea	flint	flounce	fluorescent
flammable	fleck	flip	flounder	fluoride
flank	fledgling	flippant	flour	flurry
flannel	flee	flirt	flourish	flush
flap	fleece	flit	flout	flute
flare	fleet	float	flow	flutter
flash	flesh	flock	flower	flux

CONSONANT BLENDS

FR-

fracas	frantic	freight	frill	front
fraction	fraternal	frenzy	fringe	frontier
fracture	fraud	frequent	frisk	frost
fragile	fraught	fresh	fritter	frosty
fragment	fray	fret	frivolous	froth
fragrance	frazzle	friar	frizz	frown
fragrant	freak	friction	frizzle	frozen
frail	freckle	fried	frock	frugal
frame	free	friend	frog	fruit
franc	freedom	frigate	frolic	frustrate
franchise	freeze	fright	from	fry
frank	freezer	frigid	frond	

GL-

glacial	gland	glib	gloat	glossary
glacier	glare	glide	glob	glove
glad	glass	glider	globe	glow
glade	glaze	glimmer	gloom	glucose
gladiator	gleam	glimpse	glorious	glue
gladly	glean	glint	glory	glum
glamour	glee	glisten	gloss	glut
glance	glen	glitter		glutton
				glycerin

GR-

grab	graph	grid	grin	gross
grace	graphic	griddle	grind	grouch
gracious	grapple	grief	grinder	ground
grade	grasp	grievance	grip	group
gradual	grass	grieve	gripe	grouse
graduate	grate	griffin	grisly	grove
graduation	grateful	grill	gristle	grovel
graft	gratify	grim	grit	grow
grain	gratis	grime	gritty	growl
gram	gratitude	grimy	grizzly	grown
grammar	grave	great	groan	growth
granary	gravel	greatly	grocer	grudge
grand	gravity	greed	grog	gruel
granite	gravy	green	groggy	gruff
grant	gray	greet	groin	grumble
granular	graze	grenade	groom	grumpy
grape	grease	grew	groove	grunt
grapefruit	greasy	grey	grope	

CONSONANT BLENDS

PL-

placard	plant	plea	ploy
placate	planter	plead	pluck
place	plaque	pleasant	plug
placement	plasma	please	plum
placid	plaster	pleasure	plumage
plaque	plastic	pleat	plumb
plaid	plate	pledge	plumber
plain	plateau	plentiful	plume
plaint	platform	plenty	plummet
plaintiff	platinum	pliable	plump
plait	platoon	pliant	plunder
plan	platter	pliers	plunge
plane	platypus	plight	plunger
planet	plausible	plod	plunk
plank	play	plop	plural
plankton	player	plot	plus
planner	plaza	plow	plush
			ply

PR-

practical	prestige	privilege	promise
practice	pretend	prize	promote
prairie	pretty	probable	prompt
praise	preview	probably	prone
prance	prey	probe	prong
prank	price	problem	pronounce
prattle	prick	proceed	proof
prawn	prickle	process	prop
pray	pride	procession	propel
prayer	priest	proclaim	proper
preach	prim	produce	property
precinct	prime	profess	propose
precious	primitive	profession	prose
precise	primp	professor	protect
predict	prince	profile	protest
prefer	princess	profit	proud
premise	principal	profound	prove
prepare	print	profuse	prow
present	prior	program	prowl
preserve	prism	progress	prude
president	prison	prohibit	prudent
press	private	project	prune
pressure		prom	pry

CONSONANT BLENDS

SCH-

schedule
scheme
scholar
scholarship
scholastic
school
schooner

SCR-

scrag
scrap
scrape
scratch
scrawl
scrawny
scream
screech
screen
screw
scribble
scribe
scrim
scrimmage
scrimp
script
scrub
scruple
scrutiny

SHR-

shrank
shrapnel
shred
shrew
shrewd
shriek
shrift
shrike
shrill
shrimp
shrine
shrink
shrive
shrivel
shroud
shrub
shrug
shrunk

SK-

skate
skeleton
skeptic
sketch
skew
skewer
ski
skid
skiff
skill
skim
skimp
skin
skip
skirmish
skirt
skit
skulk
skull
skunk
sky

SL-

slab
slack
slacks
slag
slain
slake
slalom
slam
slander
slang
slant
slap
slapstick
slash
slat
slate
slaughter
slave
slavery

slaw
slay
sleazy
sled
sledge
sleek
sleep
sleepy
sleet
sleeve
sleigh
sleight
slender
slept
sleuth
slew
slice
slicer
slick

slicker
slid
slide
slight
slim
slime
sling
slink
slip
slipper
slit
slither
sliver
slob
slobber
slogan
sloop
slop
slope

sloppy
slosh
slot
sloth
slouch
slovenly
slow
sludge
slug
slugger
sluice
slum
slumber
slump
slung
slunk
slur
slurp
slush
sly

18

CONSONANT BLENDS

SM-

smack	smile	smitten	smote
smart	smirch	smock	smother
smash	smirk	smog	smudge
smear	smit	smoke	smug
smell	smite	smolder	smuggle
smelt	smith	smooth	smut

SN-

snack	sneak	snipe	snout
snail	sneer	snivel	snow
snake	sneeze	snob	snub
snap	snicker	snoop	snuff
snare	sniff	snooze	snuffle
snarl	sniffle	snore	snug
snatch	snip	snort	snuggle

SP-

spa	special	spindle	spud
space	species	spine	spume
spade	specific	spinet	spunk
span	speck	spire	spur
spangle	speckle	spirit	spurt
spank	sped	spit	sputter
spar	speech	spite	spy
spare	speed	spittle	
spark	spell	spoil	
sparkle	spend	spoke	
sparrow	spent	sponge	
sparse	spew	spool	
spasm	splice	spoon	
spat	spider	spoor	
spatter	spike	sport	
spawn	spill	spot	
speak	split	spouse	
spear	spin	spout	

SPL-

splash	spleen	splice	splotch
splatter	splendid	splint	splurge
splay	splendor	split	splutter

CONSONANT BLENDS

SPR-

sprain	spray	spring	sprout
sprang	spread	sprinkle	spruce
sprat	spree	sprint	sprung
sprawl	sprig	sprit	spry

SQU-

squab	squander	squeak	squib
squabble	square	squeal	squid
squad	squash	squeamish	squint
squalid	squat	squeeze	squire
squall	squaw	squelch	squirm
squalor			squirt

ST-

stab	start	step	stork
stable	starve	sterile	storm
stack	stash	stern	story
stadium	state	stew	stout
staff	static	stick	stove
stag	status	stiff	stow
stage	staunch	stifle	stub
stagger	stave	still	stubble
stagnant	stay	stilt	stud
staid	stead	sting	student
stain	steady	stink	stuff
stair	steal	stint	stumble
stake	stealth	stir	stump
stale	steam	stitch	stun
stalk	steed	stock	stung
stall	steel	stair	stunt
stamp	steep	stole	stupid
stand	steeple	stone	sturdy
staple	steer	stood	sty
star	stein	stop	style
starch	stem	store	
stark			

STR-

straddle	straw	strew	stroke
strafe	stray	strict	stroll
straight	streak	stride	strong
strain	stream	strife	strove
strait	street	strike	struggle
strand	strength	string	strut
strangle	stress	strip	
strap	stretch	strike	

CONSONANT BLENDS

SW-

swab	swat	swept	swirl
swag	swath	swift	swish
swain	sway	swig	switch
swallow	swear	swill	swivel
swam	sweat	swim	swoop
swamp	sweep	swindle	sworn
swan	sweet	swine	
swap	swell	swing	
swarm	swelter	swipe	

TR-

trace	trapper	tribute	trooper
track	trash	trick	trophy
tract	trashy	trickle	tropic
traction	travel	tricky	tropical
tractor	traverse	tried	trot
trade	trawl	trifle	trouble
tradition	trawler	trigger	trough
traffic	tray	trillion	trounce
tragedy	tread	trim	trout
tragic	treason	trio	truce
trail	treat	trip	truck
trailer	treaty	tripe	trudge
train	tree	triple	true
trainer	trek	tripod	truly
trait	tremble	trite	trump
traitor	tremor	triumph	trumpet
tramp	trench	trivet	trundle
trample	trend	trivia	trunk
trance	trespass	trivial	truss
transfer	tress	trod	trust
transit	trestle	troll	trusty
transmit	trial	trolley	truth
trap	triangle	trombone	try
trapeze	tribe	troop	tryst

TW-

twang	twentieth	twin	twist
tweak	twenty	twine	twit
tweed	twice	twinge	twitch
tweezers	twiddle	twinkle	twitter
twelfth	twig	twinkling	
twelve	twilight	twirl	

CONSONANT BLENDS/FINAL

-DGE

abridge	cadge		ledge	sedge
adjudge	dodge	fudge	lodge	sledge
alledge	dredge	grudge	misjudge	sludge
badge	drudge	hedge	nudge	smudge
bridge	edge	judge	pledge	trudge
budge	fledge	kedge	ridge	wedge

-FT

			-LK	
adrift	gift	shift	bilk	milk
aft	graft	soft	bulk	silk
aloft	haft	swift	elk	sulk
cleft	left	theft	hulk	walk
craft	lift	thrift		
daft	loft	tuft		
deft	oft	waft		
draft	raft	weft		
drift	rift			

-NT

absent	event	hint	pint	sent
annoint	extent	hunt	plant	shunt
appoint	faint	indent	point	slant
ant	flaunt	invent	print	spent
aunt	flint	jaunt	punt	sprint
bent	footprint	joint	quaint	squint
blunt	fount	lent	rant	stint
brunt	front	lint	rent	stunt
bunt	gent	mint	resent	taunt
cent	glint	mount	runt	tent
chant	grant	paint	saint	tint
dent	grunt	pant	scant	vent
dint	haunt	pent	scent	want
				went

-ND

abscond	bond	gland	mound	spend
and	bound	grand	pond	stand
around	brand	grind	pound	strand
band	command	ground	rand	tend
bend	end	hand	refund	trend
behind	fend	hind	remind	vend
beyond	find	hound	rend	wand
bind	fond	kind	rind	wind
bland	found	land	rotund	withstand
blend	friend	lend	round	wound
blind	frond	mend	send	
blond	fund	mind	sound	

CONSONANT BLENDS/FINAL

-NG

bang	dong	king	rung	stung
bing	dung	long	sang	sung
bong	fang	lung	sing	swing
bring	fling	pang	slang	ting
clang	gang	ping	sling	wing
cling	gong	pong	sprang	wrong
clung	hang	prong	spring	zing
ding	hung	rang	sting	

-NK

bank	dank	honk	prank	stank
blank	drank	junk	rank	stink
blink	drink	kink	rink	stunk
bonk	drunk	lank	sank	sunk
brink	dunk	link	shank	swank
bunk	fink	mink	sink	tank
clank	flank	pink	slink	wink
clink	flunk	plank	slunk	zonk
clunk	frank	plink	spank	
crank	hank	plunk	spunk	

-PT

abrupt	apt	erupt	opt	swept
accept	corrupt	except	prompt	wept
adapt	crept	inept	rapt	wrapt
adept	crept	interrupt	sept	
adopt	disrupt	kept	slept	

-SP   ## -ST

asp	aghast	dust	last	roast
clasp	beast	east	least	rust
crisp	best	exist	lest	test
gasp	blast	fast	list	thirst
grasp	blest	feast	lost	toast
hasp	boast	fest	mast	trust
lisp	breast	fist	mist	tryst
rasp	bust	frost	most	vast
wasp	cast	ghost	must	vest
wisp	chest	gist	nest	west
	coast	grist	past	wrest
	cost	guest	pest	wrist
	crest	gust	post	yeast
	crust	heist	priest	zest
	cyst	host	quest	
	disgust	jest	rest	

23

CH-

chafe	chapter	cheese	chip
chain	charcoal	cherry	chipmunk
chair	charge	chess	chirp
chaise	chariot	chest	chive
chalk	charm	chew	chocolate
challenge	charming	chick	choice
chamber	chase	chicken	choke
champ	chat	chief	chop
champion	chatter	child	chubby
chance	cheap	chill	chuck
change	cheat	chilly	chum
channel	check	chime	chunk
chant	checker	chimney	church
chap	cheek	chin	churn
chapel	cheer	china	

KN-

PH-		TH- (then)

knack	phalanx	phoebe	than
knapsack	phantasm	phoenix	that
knave	phantom	phone	the
knead	pharmacist	phonics	thee
knee	pharmacy	phonograph	their
kneel	pharynx	phony	them
knell	phase	phosphate	themselves
knelt	pheasant	photo	then
knew	phenomenal	photograph	thence
knickknack	philanthropy	phrase	there
knife	philosopher	physic	these
knight	philosophy	physical	they
knit	phlegm	physician	thine
knob	phlegmatic	physics	this
knock	phlox	physiology	those
knoll	phobia	physique	thou
knot			though
know			thus
knowledge			thy
known			
knuckle			

TH- (thin)

thane	thigh	thorny	thrive
thank	thimble	thorough	throat
thankful	thin	thought	throb
thatch	thing	thousand	throne
theater	think	thrash	throttle
theft	third	thread	through
theme	thirst	threat	throw
thermal	thirsty	three	thrust
thermometer	thirty	threw	thud
thesis	thistle	thrice	thug
thick	thong	thrift	thumb
thief	thorn	thrill	thump
			thunder

CONSONANT DIGRAPHS/INITIAL

WR-

wrack	wriggle
wraith	wright
wrangle	wring
wrap	wrinkle
wrath	wrist
wreak	writ
wreath	write
wreck	writhe
wren	wrong
wrench	wrote
wrest	wrought
wrestle	wrung
wretch	wry

QU-

quack	quest
quaff	question
quail	quibble
quaint	quick
quake	quiet
qualm	quill
quarry	quilt
quart	quince
quartz	quip
quaver	quirk
quay	quite
queasy	quiver
queen	quiz
queer	quoit
quell	quota
quench	quote
query	

WH-

whack	when	whimsical	whist
whale	whence	whine	whistle
wharf	where	whinny	white
what	whether	whip	whither
wheat	whey	whir	whittle
wheedle	which	whirl	whoa
wheel	whiff	whisk	whopper
wheeze	while	whisker	whorl
whelp	whim	whisper	why

CONSONANT DIGRAPHS/MEDIAL OR FINAL

PH-

alphabet	elephant	nymph	trophy
autograph	gopher	orphan	typhoid
dolphin	nephew	triumph	typhoon

CONSONANT DIGRAPH/FINAL

-CH

arch	brunch	ditch	latch	preach	switch
attach	bunch	drench	leech	punch	teach
batch	catch	each	lunch	reach	thatch
beach	church	epoch	march	pitch	touch
beech	cinch	fetch	match	poach	twitch
bench	clench	finch	much	search	vetch
beseech	clinch	fletch	munch	scratch	watch
birch	clutch	flinch	notch	screech	wench
bitch	coach	hatch	perch	sketch	which
bleach	couch	hitch	pinch	snatch	witch
blotch	crotch	hutch	pitch	speech	wrench
botch	crunch	graph	poach	splotch	wretch
breach	crutch	impeach	parch	starch	
breech	detach	inch	patch	stich	
broach	dispatch	itch	peach	stretch	

-CK

					-GH	-LK
back	fleck	pack	snack	cough	balk
black	flick	peck	sock	enough	bilk
block	flock	pick	speck	laugh	bulk
brick	frock	pluck	stack	rough	calk
buck	hack	pock	stick	tough	caulk
check	hick	prick	stock	trough	chalk
chick	hock	puck	struck		elk
chuck	jack	quack	stuck		folk
clack	kick	quick	suck		hulk
click	knack	rack	tack		milk
clock	knock	rock	thick		silk
cluck	lack	sack	tick		stalk
cock	lick	shack	track		sulk
crack	lock	shock	treck		walk
crick	luck	shuck	trick		whelk
crock	mock	sick	truck		
deck	muck	slack	tuck		
dock	neck	smack	whack		
duck	nick	smock	wick		

-SH

			-TH		
abash	flesh	rash	aftermath	hath	quoth
afresh	flush	rush	bath	health	sheath
ash	fresh	sash	beneath	heath	sixth
bash	gash	shush	birth	herewith	sloth
blush	gnash	slash	both	lath	smith
brash	gush	slosh	breath	length	south
brush	hash	slush	broth	loth	strength
bush	hush	smash	cloth	math	teeth
cash	lash	splash	death	month	troth
clash	lush	squash	depth	moth	wealth
crash	mash	squish	fifth	mouth	width
crush	mesh	stash	filth	mirth	with
dash	mush	swish	forth	ninth	wrath
dish	posh	thrash	froth	oath	wreath
enmesh	plush	thresh	girth	path	
fish	push	thrush	growth	pith	

HARD C

cab	canary	carol	coat	come	country
cabbage	cancel	carpet	cob	comment	coupon
cabin	candle	carrot	cobweb	common	court
cable	candy	carry	cock	company	cover
caboose	cane	cart	cocoa	compass	cow
cactus	cannon	carton	cod	concern	cozy
cage	canoe	carve	code	cone	cub
cake	canteen	case	coffee	conflict	cube
calculate	canyon	cat	coil	contain	cuff
calendar	cape	catalog	coin	contest	culture
calf	capital	catch	cold	control	curse
calm	capsule	caterpillar	collar	cook	custom
calorie	capture	caution	collect	copy	cut
came	car	cave	colony	cork	cute
camel	carbon	caw	color	corn	
camp	card	coach	colt	correct	
campus	care	coal	column	cost	
can	carnival	coast	comb	cottage	

SOFT C

cedar	cinch
ceiling	cinder
celery	cinnamon
cell	circle
cellar	cite
cement	citizen
cent	citrus
center	city
central	civil
cereal	civilization
ceremony	cycle
certain	cyclone
cider	cylinder
cigar	cymbal
cigarette	cypress
	cyst

HARD G

gab	garage	go	gray
gable	garden	goal	green
gadget	gargle	goat	grin
gage	garland	gobble	groan
gain	garlic	goggles	ground
gait	garment	gold	guarantee
galaxy	gas	golf	guard
gale	gash	gone	guess
gall	gasoline	good	guest
gallant	gate	goose	guide
gallery	gather	gopher	guilt
gallon	gauge	gorilla	guitar
gallop	gauze	gossip	gulf
galore	gave	got	gull
galoshes	gay	government	gum
gamble	gaze	gown	gun
game	glad	grade	guppy
gang	globe	grape	gutter
gape	glove	grass	guy

SOFT G

gelatin	gesture
gem	giant
general	ginger
generation	giraffe
generous	gym
gentle	gymnasium
genuine	gyp
geography	gypsy
geometry	gyrate
germ	gyroscope

-GHT LETTER GROUP

blight	flight	might	slight
bought	fought	night	sought
bright	fright	nought	thought
brought	fraught	ought	tight
caught	height	plight	weight
eight	knight	right	wright
fight	light	sight	wrought

RHYMING PAIRS

These are word pairs that can be used for vocabulary development. The pairs (usually an adjective and a noun) rhyme, and present humorous word pictures. These pairs are sometimes called "Hink Pinks."

To introduce this activity to students, the teacher might ask, "What is a Hink Pink for _____ _____?" (giving the definition words), and then wait for students to supply the rhyming pair.

Example: What is a Hink Pink for an overweight feline?
Hink Pink Answer: A **fat cat**.

The teacher might also ask students to provide the definition of a Hink Pink given.

Example: What is the definition of a **sad dad?**
Answer: An unhappy father.

A "Hink Pink" is used to denote pairs of one syllable each.
A "Hinky Pinky" is used to denote pairs of two syllables each.
A "Hinkety Pinkety" is used to denote pairs of three syllables each.

Pair	Definition
drab-cab	a dreary or dull colored taxi
race-pace	a rate of speed in a running event
black-crack	a dark crevice
glad-lad	a happy boy
bear-scare	a fright caused by a grizzly
rag-bag	a sack for cloth scraps
frail-male	a weak man
pale-whale	a pallid sea mammal
brain-strain	cerebral overwork
fake-snake	a fradulent reptile
chalk-talk	a blackboard discussion
sham-ram	a fake male sheep
damp-camp	a wet tentground
chance-glance	a lucky glimpse
clap-trap	a trick to win applause
grim-hymn	a stern church song
limp-blimp	a dirigible with no air
thin-fin	a fish's narrow "wing"
fine-pine	excellent grade spruce tree
pink-drink	a light red beverage
bright-light	brilliant illumination
brighter-writer	a smarter author
wise-prize	an intelligent award
dock-lock	a key-operated fastening to secure a pier
cold-gold	a cool yellow precious metal
stone-bone	a petrified femur
long-song	a lengthy tune
rude-dude	a crude guy
book-crook	a manuscript thief
broom-room	a closet for storing a sweeping tool
prune-spoon	a utensil used to eat dried plums
loose-noose	a hangman's knot that is not tight

RHYMING PAIRS

Pair	Definition
harsh-marsh	a rough and unpleasant swamp
smart-start	an intelligent beginning
last-blast	the final explosion
great-date	a wonderful appointment
bath-path	a trail to the shower
fraud-abroad	trickery overseas
brave-slave	a courageous servant
fall-brawl	an autumn fight
wax-tax	a levy on polish
clay-tray	a carrying device made of an earthen material
beach-speech	a talk at the seashore
weak-Greek	a feeble man from Greece
steel-wheel	an iron steering device
dream-scream	a nightmare cry or yell
beast-feast	a monster's banquet
sweet-treat	a sugary feast
deck-check	a ship's flooring inspection
red-shed	a crimson shack
free-bee	a honey-making insect that doesn't cost anything
cheap-sheep	an inexpensive lamb
hen-pen	a cage for chickens
bent-cent	a crooked penny
tent-rent	money paid for canvas lodging
terse-verse	a concise rhyme
wet-pet	a damp domestic animal
blue-hue	an aqua shade
tribe-scribe	the note taker for an Indian group
nice-price	a fair cost
crop-flop	failure of a farm's produce
rope-soap	detergent for cleaning heavy line
floor-store	a shop where flooring is purchased
pork-fork	a utensil to eat pig meat
cross-boss	an angry employer
host-boast	a party giver's bragging
loud-crowd	a noisy group
sound-hound	a healthy dog
flower-shower	a rain of posies
mouse-house	a dwelling for mice
stout-scout	a fat person who is sent out to look ahead
low-blow	a punch under the beltline
slow-crow	a black bird that does not fly fast
brown-crown	a tan headpiece for a ruling person
duck-truck	a vehicle for transporting waterfowl
mud-flood	an inundation of water and dirt
fudge-judge	a person who must choose the best chocolate candy
glum-chum	a sad or unhappy friend
fun-run	an enjoyable jog
tall-wall	a high stone fence
skunk-bunk	a bed for a smelly mammal
time-chime	an hour bell
pig-wig	a hog's hair piece
funny-bunny	a humorous rabbit
pure-cure	untainted medicine
mute-lute	a soundless pear-shaped stringed instrument
cute-newt	an attractive land salamander
quick-pick	a rapid selection
dry-fly	a bothersome insect that is not wet

V-CV/OPEN SYLLABLE WORDS

agent	decide	futile	minus	silence
baby	defeat	genius	miser	siphon
bacon	defend	glacier	moment	sober
baker	dilate	gopher	motel	soda
basis	diner	gyrate	nature	solo
before	eject	haven	navy	spiral
below	elect	hero	omit	spoken
blatant	erase	hobo	open	tiger
bonus	evade	hotel	oval	vacant
cedar	even	ibex	pilot	vapor
chosen	evil	ibis	polo	veto
cider	fatal	icy	quaver	vocal
climate	favor	label	radar	wager
clover	fever	labor	razor	yodel
cocoa	fiber	lady	recent	zebra
cohort	final	local	recess	zero
cycle	flavor	locate	require	
decay	frozen	major		

VC-CV/CLOSED SYLLABLE WORDS

admit	fifteen	lancer	plastic	tennis
appoint	foggy	letter	problem	tractor
ballad	follow	lumber	public	traffic
bamboo	ginger	master	quagmire	trigger
bandit	goblin	member	question	tunnel
better	gossip	metric	quitter	ulcer
bonnet	hobby	motto	rascal	umpire
cactus	hollow	muffin	rescue	under
candy	ignite	napkin	robber	upper
cotton	imbed	nectar	rubber	vampire
daddy	index	number	silver	velvet
dentist	issue	nutmeg	splendid	victor
disgust	jelly	object	splinter	welcome
doctor	jobber	offer	suffer	western
dummy	justice	optic	summer	whisper
effort	kennel	picnic	supper	window
endure	kitten	pillow	tamper	yellow
fancy	ladder	pistol	temper	yonder
				zipper

amble	dibble	kindle	rattle	stubble
ample	dimple	knuckle	riddle	stumble
angle	dingle	little	ripple	subtle
ankle	dribble	mangle	rubble	suckle
apple	drizzle	mantle	ruffle	supple
babble	dwindle	meddle	rumble	tackle
baffle	fickle	middle	rumple	tangle
bangle	fiddle	mingle	saddle	tattle
battle	fizzle	mottle	sample	temple
bobble	fondle	muddle	scribble	thimble
bottle	frazzle	muffle	scuffle	thistle
bramble	freckle	mumble	scuttle	throttle
brindle	frizzle	muscle	settle	tickle
bristle	fumble	muzzle	shackle	tingle
brittle	gamble	nestle	shingle	tipple
bubble	gentle	nettle	shuffle	topple
buckle	giggle	nibble	shuttle	trample
bundle	gobble	niggle	sickle	tremble
bungle	grapple	nimble	simple	trestle
bustle	griddle	nipple	single	trickle
cackle	grumble	nozzle	sizzle	truckle
candle	haggle	nuzzle	smuggle	truffle
castle	handle	paddle	snaffle	trundle
cattle	heckle	pebble	sniffle	tumble
chuckle	bobble	pestle	snuffle	twiddle
cobble	huddle	pickle	snuggle	twinkle
cockle	humble	piddle	spangle	uncle
coddle	hustle	pimple	sparkle	wabble
crackle	jangle	prattle	spindle	waddle
cripple	jiggle	prickle	spittle	waffle
crumble	jingle	puddle	sprinkle	waggle
crumple	joggle	puzzle	squiggle	whittle
cuddle	jostle	quibble	stickle	wimple
dabble	juggle	rabble	straddle	wiggle
dangle	jumble	raffle	strangle	wrangle
dapple	jungle	ramble	straggler	wrestle
dazzle	kettle	rankle	struggle	wrinkle
				wriggle

able	cable	gable	sable	stifle
beadle	cradle	idle	scruple	table
beagle	cycle	ladle	sidle	title
beetle	eagle	maple	stable	treacle
bridle	fable	people	staple	trifle
bugle	feeble	rifle	steeple	wheedle

a-, ab- (away from)

abide
abloom
abnormal
abode
abound

ante- (before)

antecede
antechamber
antenatal
antepenult
anteroom
antetype

anti- (against)

antibacterial
antibody
anticatalyst
anticlerical
antifreeze
antitank
antitoxin
antiwar

auto- (self)

autobiography
autobus
autoharp
autohypnosis
automobile

bi- (two)

bicycle
bimetal
bimonthly
bipolar
biweekly

circu- (around)

circumnavigate
circumpolar
circumscribe

co- (together, with)

cobelligerants
coefficient
coexist
cohabit
coheir

counter- (against)

counteract
counterattack
counterbalance
counterclaim
counterculture
counterrevolution
counterspy
counterweight

de- (away, down)

deactivate
debar
debase
debrief
decamp
degrade
dehumidify
delouse

dis- (apart from, not)

disallow
disappoint
disarm
discontinue
discount
discredit
disenchant
dislocate
disobey

ex- (from)

excogitate
excommunicate
exfoliate
exsanguinate

extra- (outside, beyond)
extracurricular
extragalactic
extrajudical
extralegal
extraordinary
extrasensory
extraterritorial

fore- (in front)

forearm
forebode
forecastle
forefinger
forefoot
forefront
foreground
forehand
forehead
foremast

PREFIXES

il- (not)

illegal
illegible
illiterate
illogical

im- (not)

immaterial
immature
immeasurable
imperfect
impersonal
impolite
improper
impure

in- (not)

inaccessible
inactive
inarticulate
inclement
incomplete
inconvenient
independent
indifferent
indirect
insane

inter- (between, among)

interact
intercede
interchange
intercontinental
intermingle
intermix
intersection
interstellar

ir- (not)

irradiate
irrational
irregular
irrelevant
irreligious
irreplaceable
irrepressable
irresponsible
irreverent
irreversible

mid- (middle)

midair
midday
midland
midnight
midpoint
midships
midsummer

mis- (wrong)

misadventure
misapply
miscast
miscue
misfortune
misname
misspell
misstep
misunderstand

non- (not)

nonabrasive
nonburnable
nonconductor
nondurable
nonentity
nonsmoker
nonviolent
nonvocal
nonvoter
nonunion

over- (over)

overactive
overbold
overcharge
overdress
overgrown
overlay
overpay
overreact
overrun
overtax

post- (after)

postdate
postoperative
postscript
postwar

pre- (before)

precaution
preclude
precursor
predate
predict
prefabricate
prefix
premarital
prepay
presume

pro- (before, in front, forward, forth)

procreate
produce
profess
profile
profound
project
pronoun
provoke

re- (again)

reclaim
redo
refinish
reline
relive
remount
repaint
replace

sub- (under)

subdivide
submarine
subnormal
subplot
subsoil
substandard
suburban

super- (over)

supercede
supercharge
superego
superhighway
superhuman
superman
supernatural
supermarket
supernova

tele- (far away)

telegram
telegraph
telephone
telephoto
telescope
television

trans- (across)

translucent
transmigrate
transplant
transpolar
transport
transpose

un- (not)

unclear
uneven
unfair
unfit
unglue
unhook
unlace
unlock
unpack
untie
untouched

uni- (one)

unicellular
unicycle
unilateral

SUFFIXES

-able
(tending to, able to)

conquerable
enjoyable
lovable
payable
perishable
readable
reliable
washable

-age
(state of being)
(place of, result of)

anchorage
orphanage
parsonage
personage
shrinkage
wastage

-al
(relating to)

commercial
electrical
residential
technical
theatrical

-ance, -ence
(state of being)

allowance
attendance
difference
excellence
importance

-ary, -ery
(that which, place where)

bakery
cannery
creamery
dictionary
forgery
nursery
revolutionary

-en
(having nature of)

ashen
broken
earthen
fallen
golden
molten
spoken
swollen
wooden
woven

-en
(to make or become)

blacken
fatten
flatten
lengthen
roughen
shorten
straighten
whiten
widen

-er
(one who, that which)

baker
carpenter
cleaner
foreigner
grocer
jumper
preacher
runner
teacher
worker

-er
(more "in degree")

faster
fatter
lighter
nicer
sicker
shorter
slower
smarter
stronger
taller

-est
(most "in degree")

cleanest
deepest
easiest
farthest
latest
longest
loudest
skinniest
tightest
widest

-ful
(characterized by, full of)

awful
beautiful
graceful
helpful
masterful
plentiful
skillful
successful
thankful
wonderful

-fy
(make or form into)

clarify
glorify
horrify
identify
justify
modify
notify
qualify
simplify
testify

-hood
(state of rank)

adulthood
boyhood
brotherhood
childhood
falsehood
maidenhood
manhood
neighborhood
priesthood
womanhood

-ic
(pertaining to, like)

angelic
artistic
athletic
atmospheric
classic
critic
dramatic
historic
volcanic

SUFFIXES

-ive
(having nature of
quality of, given to)

active
corrective
destructive
effective
explosive
festive
impressive
inventive
protective

-ity, -ty
(state of being)

acidity
purity
reality
sovereignty

-ist
(one who)

artist
biologist
botonist
communist
humorist
journalist
loyalist
optomist
pessimist
pianist

-ish
(having
nature of)

bluish
childish
clownish
fiendish
foolish
sickish
sixish
whitish

-less
(without)

ageless
childless
fatherless
graceless
helpless
hopeless
merciless
penniless
priceless
witless
worthless

-ly
(in the
manner of)

actively
attentively
happily
justly
patiently
quietly
rapidly
sadly
silently
swiftly

-ment
(resulting state,
action or process)

amazement
commitment
employment
movement
payment
placement
punishment
refinement
settlement
treatment

-most
(most "in degree")

aftermost
bottommost
foremost
furthermost
hindmost
innermost
northernmost
outermost
topmost

-ness
(quality or
state of being)

blindness
gladness
goodness
kindness
likeness
sickness
sweetness
thickness
weakness
wickedness

-or
(person who,
state of quality)

actor
auditor
creditor
debtor
executor
supervisor

-ous
(state or condition,
having quality of)

courageous
dangerous
humorous
joyous
nervous
prosperous

-ship
(office, profession
art, or skill)

championship
fellowship
friendship
hardship
horsemanship
marksmanship
partnership
penmanship
relationship
sportsmanship

-tion, -ion
(act, process,
state)

action
attraction
collection
correction
dictation
education
election
narration
protection
rejection

-ure
(act, process)

adventure
composure
enclosure
failure
pleasure

CONTRACTIONS

aren't
can't
couldn't
didn't
doesn't
don't
hadn't
hasn't
haven't
he'd
he'll
he's
here's
I'd
I'll
I'm
isn't
it's
I've
let's
mustn't

she'd
she'll
she's
shouldn't
that's
there's
they'd
they'll
they're
wasn't
we'd
we'll
we're
weren't
what's
where's
who'd
who's
won't
wouldn't
you'll
you're
you've

PREPOSITIONS

about
above
across
after
along
among
amongst
around
as
at
before
behind
below
beside
between
by
down
for
from
in
inside
into
like
of
off
on
onto
out
outside
over
through
to
toward
under
underneath
until
up
upon
with
within

CONJUNCTIONS

Co-ordinating

and
but
for
nor
or
so
yet

Subordinating

after
because
if
since
till
when
where
while

COMPOUND WORDS

afternoon
airline
airplane
alongside
anybody
anyone
anyplace
anything
anytime
anyway
anywhere
arrowhead
backbone
backyard
baseball
baseman
basketball
bathrobe
bathroom
bathtub
bedroom
bedtime
beehive
birdbath
blackboard
blacksmith
boathouse
boldface
broomstick
buckskin
businessmen
butterfly
campfire
campground
candlestick
cannot
catfish
chairman
chalkboard
checkerboard
cheeseburger
classmate
classroom
coastline
coffeepot
commonplace
corncob
cornfield

countryman
countryside
courthouse
courtyard
cowboy
craftsman
crossbow
daybreak
daytime
dishpan
doorbell
doorway
downhill
downstairs
downstream
downtown
driftwood
driveway
drugstore
dugout
earthquake
eggshell
elsewhere
everybody
everyday
everyone
everything
everywhere
eyebrow
eyelid
farewell
farmhouse
farmland
fingerprint
fireman
firewood
fireworks
flagpole
flashlight
flowerpot
football
footprint
footstep
forget
framework
freshman
furthermore
gingerbread

goldfish
grandfather
grandmother
grasshopper
grassland
hairbrush
halfway
handkerchief
handshake
handwriting
headdress
headline
highlands
highway
hillside
homeland
homemade
homework
hopscotch
horseback
horseman
horseshoe
hourglass
houseboat
household
housewife
however
icebox
indoor
inland
inside
intake
into
junkyard
landmark
landowner
lifetime
lighthouse
lightweight
limestone
lookout
lowlands
mailbox
mainland
moonlight
mountainside

newspaper
nightfall
nobody
northeast
northwest
notebook
nothing
nowhere
offspring
otherwise
outcome
outdoors
outline
outside
overall
overcome
overhead
overlook
overnight
paintbrush
pancake
playground
policeman
popcorn
proofread
quarterback
raincoat
raindrop
rainfall
railroad
railway
rattlesnake
roadside
rowboat
runaway
runway

sailboat
salesman
sandstone
scarecrow
schoolhouse
schoolroom
scrapbook
seaport
seashell
seashore
seaweed
sidewalk
snowball
snowflake
snowman
somebody
someday
somehow
someone
something
sometime
somewhat
somewhere
southeast
southwest
spaceship
springtime
stagecoach
stairway
starfish
steamboat
storekeeper
suitcase
summertime
sundown
sunlight
sunrise
sunset
sunshine

textbook
themselves
thereafter
throughout
townspeople
treetop
typewriter
undergo
underground
underline
underlying
underside
understand
underwater
upright
upstream
vineyard
warehouse
waterfall
waterway
weekend
whatever
whenever
whereas
wherever
whoever
widespread
wildlife
windmill
withdraw
within
without
woodland
worthwhile
yourself

A.D.	Anno Domini, in the year of our Lord		elem.	elementary
ad., adv.	advertisement		enc.	enclosure
A.M., a.m.	ante meridiem, before noon		enc.	encyclopedia
Amer.	America; American		Eng.	English
anon.	anonymous		Esq.	Esquire
apt.	apartment		E.S.T.	Eastern Standard Time
assn.	association		etc.	et cetera, and so forth
assoc.	associate; associated		F	Fahrenheit
asst.	assistant		FBI	Federal Bureau of Investigation
atty.	attorney			
ave.	avenue		FDA	Food and Drug Administration
B.A.	Bachelor of Arts		fig.	figure
B.C.	Before Christ; British Columbia		Fr.	Father; Friar; French
bibliog.	bibliography		Fri.	Friday
bldg.	building		ft.	feet; foot; fort
blvd.	boulevard		gal.	gallon
bros.	brothers		geog.	geography
bur.	bureau		Gov.	Governor
C	Centigrade; Celcius		govt.	government
cal.	calories		grad.	graduate; graduated
cap.	capital		gr.	gram
cdr.	commander		hdqrs.	headquarters
cent.	century		Heb.	Hebrew; Hebrews
ch., chap.	chapter		hist.	historical; history
chm.	chairman		Hon.	Honorable
cm.	centimeter		ht.	height; heat
c/o	care of		I., i.	island
co.	company; county		ibid.	ibidem, in the same place
c.o.d.	cash on delivery collect on delivery		ill., illus.	illustration
coll.	college; collection		inc.	incorporated; including
conf.	conference		in.	inch
Cont.	Continental		incog.	incognito (unknown)
cont.	continued		Ind.	Indian; Indiana
coop.	cooperative		ins.	insurance
cop, ©	copyright		int.	interest; international
corp.	corporation		intro.	introduction
C.S.T.	Central Standard Time		I.O.U.	I owe you
D.A.	District Attorney		I.Q.	intelligence quotient
DDT	dichloro-diphenyl-trichloroethane		Jr.	Junior
Dem.	Democrat		junc.	junction
dept.	department		kg.	kilogram
diag.	diagram		km.	kilometer
dict.	dictionary		l.	liter
dm.	decimeter		lab.	laboratory
doz.	dozen		lang.	language
Dr.	doctor		lat.	latitude
D.S.T.	Daylight Saving Time		lb.	pound
ed.	edition		leg.	legislature
educ.	education		lib.	librarian; library
			liq.	liquid
			lit.	literature
			Lt., Lieut.	Lieutenant

Ltd., Lim.	Limited
m.	meter
M.A.	Master of Arts
math	mathematics
max.	maximum
M.D.	Doctor of Medicine
mdse.	merchandise
meas.	measure
memo	memorandum
mfg.	manufacturing
mfr., manuf.	manufacturer
min.	minute
misc.	miscellaneous
Mlle.	Mademoiselle
mi.	mile
mml.	millimeter
Mme.	Madame
mo.	month
Mon.	Monday
mph	miles per hour
Msgr.	Monsignor
Mr.	Mister
Mrs.	Mistress
M.S.T.	Mountain Standard Time
Mt., mt.	Mount; mountain
mun.	municipal
myth	mythology
n.	noun; north
nat., natl.	national
NATO	North Atlantic Treaty Organization
no.	number
O.K.	correct; all right
oz.	ounce
p.	page
par.	paragraph; parenthesis
parl.	parliament
pat.	patent
pd.	paid
per cent	per centum
Ph.D.	Doctor of Philosophy
philos.	philosophy
phot., photog.	photograph
pk.	park; peak; peck
pl.	plural; place; plate
P.M., p.m.	post meridiem, after noon; postmaster; post mortem
P.O.	post office
pop.	population
POW	prisoner of war
ppd.	prepaid
Pres.	President
prin.	principal
Prof.	Professor
prop.	property
Prov.	Proverbs
P.S.	post scriptum, postscript
P.S.T.	Pacific Standard Time
pt.	pint
qt.	quart
rd.	road
recd.	received
ref.	reference; refer
reg.	region; regulation
regt.	regiment
rep.	representative; republic
Rev.	Reverend; Revelations
rev.	review; revise; revolution
R.I.P.	rest in peace
R.R.	railroad
R.S.V.P.	Answer, if you please
Ry.	railway
Sat.	Saturday
sch.	school
sec.	second
secy.	secretary
sig.	signature
sing.	singular
sp.	spelling; species; space
spec.	specification
sq.	square
Sr.	Senior
St.	Saint; strait; street
subj.	subject
Sun.	Sunday
Supt.	Superintendent
syn.	synonym
t.	ton
tech.	technical; technology
temp.	temperature
Thurs.	Thursday
treas.	treasurer
Tues.	Tuesday
UN	United Nations
univ.	university
v.	verb
v, vs	versus, against
vet.	veteran; veterinary
VIP	Very Important Person
vol.	volume
V.P.	Vice-President
Wed.	Wednesday
wk.	week
wt.	weight
Xmas	Christmas
yd.	yard
yr.	year

SELECTED WORD LIST

Word	Synonym	Antonym	Homonym
above	over	below	—
absent	missing	present	—
abuse	mistreat	abet	—
add	total	subtract	—
adept	proficient	unskilled	—
adore	love	hate	—
advance	proceed	retreat	—
aid	help	hinder	ade, aide
air	atmosphere	earth	heir
aisle	passageway	blockade	isle
alike	same	different	—
all	everything	none	awl
alter	change	preserve	—
ancient	old	modern	—
answer	reply	question	—
appear	emerge	disappear	—
arid	dry	wet	—
ate	consumed	fasted	eight
attach	fasten	remove	—
aunt	—	—	ant
awake	arouse	asleep	—
baby	infant	adult	—
back	rear	front	—
backward	reversed	forward	—
bad	evil	good	—
bag	sack	box	—
bare	naked	clothed	bear
basis	foundation	summit	bases
be	exist	isn't	bee
beach	shore	ocean	beech
beat	rhythm	—	beet
beautiful	lovely	ugly	—
been	was	wasn't	bin
before	formerly	after	—
begin	start	end	—
below	beneath	above	—
bend	curve	straighten	—
black	dark	white	—
blew	gusted	calmed	blue
blunt	dull	sharp	—
boat	ship	—	—
bore	weary	excite	boar
*bow	submit	refuse	bough
bowl	dish	—	bole, boll
box	carton	—	—
brave	courageous	frightened	—
break	shatter	repair	brake
breath	respiration	—	breadth
bridal	wedding	—	bridle
bright	brilliant	dim	—
brink	edge	center	—
bury	inter	unearth	berry
buy	purchase	sell	by, bye
calm	tranquil	excited	—

*heteronym

41

SELECTED WORD LIST

Word	Synonym	Antonym	Homonym
canvas	fabric	paper	—
cap	hat	—	—
capital	wealth	liability	capitol
caret	insertion	deletion	carot, carrot
carpet	rug	—	—
cereal	porridge	—	serial
chief	leader	follower	—
city	metropolis	country	—
choose	select	reject	—
clever	smart	dumb	—
*close	shut	open	—
coarse	rough	smooth	course
cold	icy	hot	—
collect	gather	disperse	—
come	arrive	go	—
comic	funny	tragic	—
compliment	praise	criticise	complement
cool	chilly	warm	—
counsel	advise	ignore	council
creek	brook	—	creak
cry	weep	laugh	—
damage	injure	repair	—
danger	peril	safety	—
dark	opaque	light	—
day	daylight	night	—
dead	deceased	alive	—
dear	darling	—	deer
decrease	reduce	increase	—
deep	great	shallow	—
*desert	abandon	retrieve	dessert
despise	hate	adore	—
devour	eat	regurgitate	—
die	decease	live	dye
difficult	hard	easy	—
dirty	filthy	clean	—
disperse	distribute	gather	—
distant	far	near	—
dry	arid	wet	—
dull	boring	exciting	—
early	premature	late	—
elusive	evasive	overt	—
eminent	prominent	obscure	—
employ	hire	fire	—
empty	vacant	full	—
end	finish	begin	—
enemy	foe	friend	—
enlarge	expand	reduce	—
entice	tempt	scorn	—
error	mistake	truth	—
even	—	odd	—
exceed	excel	fail	—
except	but	—	—

*heteronym

42

SELECTED WORD LIST

Word	Synonym	Antonym	Homonym
excess	overabundance	lack	—
exit	leave	enter	—
expand	swell	contract	—
export	send	import	—
fail	flop	succeed	—
fair	just	unfair	fare
fall	descend	rise	—
fat	obese	thin	—
feat	deed	—	fete
feeble	weak	strong	—
first	foremost	last	—
fix	repair	break	—
flower	blossom	—	flour
forth	forward	back	fourth
form	shape	unformed	—
follow	pursue	lead	—
foolish	silly	wise	—
formerly	before	after	—
frighten	terrify	soothe	—
funny	humorous	serious	—
fur	pelt	—	fir
future	hereafter	past	—
gain	profit	loss	—
gamble	bet	—	gambol
gather	assemble	disburse	—
gaunt	thin	plump	—
gaze	stare	glance	—
generous	magnanimous	selfish	—
gift	present	—	—
giggle	chuckle	whimper	—
good	kind	bad	—
gorilla	ape	—	—
great	large	small	grate
groan	moan	laugh	grown
hail	—	—	hell
halt	stop	advance	—
hangar	shed	—	hanger
happy	glad	sad	—
hard	rigid	soft	—
hare	rabbit	—	hair
harmless	safe	detrimental	—
hate	despise	love	—
heal	cure	infect	heel
healthy	well	ill	—
heavy	weighty	light	—
here	present	there	hear
heroine	victor	loser	heroin
hinder	obstruct	help	—
holy	sacred	profane	wholly
homely	ugly	pretty	—
hot	heated	cold	—
huge	large	tiny	—

*heteronym

43

Word	Synonym	Antonym	Homonym
hurl	throw	catch	—
idle	slothful	busy	idol, idyll
ill	sick	well	—
illusive	phantasmal	tangible	—
imaginary	illusory	real	—
in	inside	out	inn
inflate	expand	deflate	—
iniquity	wickedness	goodness	—
innocent	faultless	guilty	—
insight	discernment	—	incite
its	—	—	it's
joy	happiness	sadness	—
keen	sharp	blunt	—
knave	rascal	gentleman	nave
knows	understands	(is) ignorant	nose
latch	lock	unbolt	—
late	tardy	early	—
leak	crack	—	leek
leave	depart	return	—
led	guided	followed	*lead
liar	deceiver	—	lyre
like	same	different	—
*live	exist	die	—
little	small	big	—
lone	one	several	loan
loose	free	tight	—
loud	noisy	quiet	—
low	inferior	high	lo
made	created	destroyed	maid
male	man	—	mail
mantle	cloak	—	mantel
medal	award	—	metal, mettle
meet	assemble	adjourn	meat
minor	petty	major	—
missle	projectile	—	missal
more	additional	less	—
mourning	grief	gladness	morning
mousse	—	—	moose
muscle	strength	weakness	mussel
narrow	limited	wide	—
native	indigenous	foreign	—
natural	normal	strange	—
naval	nautical	—	navel
neat	orderly	disarrayed	—
necessary	obligatory	unnecessary	—
need	require	have	knead
new	contemporary	old	knew, gnu
night	evening	day	—
no	negative	yes	know
noisy	loud	quiet	—
none	nothing	all	nun
not	—	—	knot
open	unfasten	close	—
our	—	—	hour

*heteronym

SELECTED WORD LIST

Word	Synonym	Antonym	Homonym
pain	ache	pleasure	pane
pair	twins	single	pare
pale	pallid	rosy	pail
pallet	—	—	palette, palate
peace	accord	war	piece
peal	ring	—	peel
pin	fasten	undo	—
place	put	remove	plaice
plain	intelligible	confusing	plane
polite	courteous	rude	—
powerful	strong	weak	—
presence	proximity	absence	*presents
prey	quarry	hunter	pray
principle	essential	unnecessary	principal
prohibit	forbid	permit	—
*project	protrude	recede	—
push	shove	pull	—
question	query	answer	—
raise	elevate	lower	raze
*read	peruse	—	reed
real	actual	fake	reel
*record	chronicle	play	—
red	florid	pale	read
*refuse	decline	accept	—
reign	rule	obey	rain
remain	stay	leave	—
rich	wealthy	poor	—
right	correct	wrong	wright, rite
ring	peal	—	wring
rock	stone	—	—
rode	drove	walked	road
rough	coarse	smooth	ruff
route	course	—	root, rout
rumor	gossip	truth	roomer
sad	unhappy	glad	—
same	identical	different	—
scene	setting	—	seen
scents	smells	—	cents
scream	yell	whisper	—
sea	ocean	—	see
seem	appear	is	seam
sell	vend	purchase	cell
sent	dispatched	returned	—
serf	slave	master	surf
sheer	thin	opaque	shear
shop	store	—	—
shy	timid	aggressive	—
sight	vision	blindness	site, cite
slay	murder	save	sleigh
sleep	slumber	wake	—
slow	dilatory	fast	sloe
small	tiny	large	—
smile	grin	frown	—
soar	fly	land	sore

*heteronym

45

SELECTED WORD LIST

Word	Synonym	Antonym	Homonym
sole	only	several	soul
some	few	many	sum
son	scion	—	sun
sour	acerbic	sweet	—
*sow	plant	reap	so, sew
speak	talk	listen	—
stake	peg	—	steak
stare	gaze	glance	stair
start	begin	stop	—
stationary	motionless	movable	stationery
steal	rob	buy	steel
straight	undeviating	curved	strait
stray	deviate	stay	—
strong	substantial	weak	—
stubborn	obstinate	yielding	—
tacks	nails	—	tax
take	steal	return	—
tale	fable	—	tail
tardy	late	punctual	—
taught	instructed	learned	taut
tea	—	—	tee
*tear	—	—	tier
there	—	here	their, they're
threw	pitched	caught	through
time	—	—	thyme
timid	afraid	assured	—
to	—	from	too, two
top	apex	bottom	—
tow	pull	push	toe
troupe	company	—	troop
true	certain	false	—
unique	original	common	—
usual	normal	rare	—
vacant	empty	full	—
vain	futile	warranted	vein, vane
vice	fault	virtue	—
wait	tarry	rush	weight
want	desire	need	won't
waste	squander	conserve	waist
wave	bellow	—	waive
way	direction	—	weigh
weak	feeble	strong	week
wear	don	—	where
well	fortuitous	ill	—
*wind	breeze	—	—
whole	entire	—	hole
whose	—	—	who's
wild	savage	tame	—
whoa	stop	go	woe
wood	lumber	—	would
won	succeeded	lost	one
wry	crooked	straight	rye
you	—	—	ewe, yew

*heteronym

IDIOMS

She bawled her eyes out.
My brother gets in my hair.
He lost his marbles.
The idea rang a bell.
He was burned up.
Go fly a kite.
He almost bit my head off!
She blew her stack.
He's on top of the world.
She is as quiet as a church mouse.
He's as neat as a pin.
The baby is prettier than a picture.
He's like a bull in a china shop.
He is as ugly as a mud fence.
Money was as scarce as hen's teeth.
That will take him down a peg.
Dad will get wind of it.
Money always burns a hole in my pocket.
Will you lend me a hand?
She was so nervous she blew the test.
I was so scared, I was shaking in my boots.
The girl was walking on air after the dance.
I was furious, but I held my tongue.
I'm between the devil and the deep blue sea.
He's not worth a hill of beans.
I think he bit off more than he can chew.
It's raining cats and dogs out there!
He has a trick up his sleeve.
It's as plain as the nose on your face.
His father is well heeled.
I'm in a pretty pickle!
Do you have a skeleton in your closet?
The handwriting was on the wall.
She can really put on the dog.
He's a stool pigeon for the police.

I'm coming, so keep your shirt on.
He's tied to his mother's apron strings.
I'll stay until the bitter end.
He's talking through his hat.
That's right down my alley.
He is a pain in the neck.
The cowboy bit the dust.
He's as nutty as a fruitcake.
I have a splitting headache.
Put your John Hancock on the paper.
I never see eye to eye with you.
Is she ever in the dumps!
For crying out loud, stop that noise.
I have a bone to pick with you!
She really can chew the fat.
You just hit the nail on the head.
By hook or by crook I'll get it.
That rings a bell with me.
The judge will throw the book at him.
Don't get your dander up.
It's nothing to shake a stick at.
Hold your horses!
I just had to blow off steam.
Keep a stiff upper lip.
I believe she is full of beans.
The teacher called him on the carpet.
That is as easy as rolling off a log.
I've got to get forty winks.
He has too many irons in the fire.
It was a long row to hoe.
She's as mad as a wet hen.
It is not fake, it's the real McCoy.
You're in the doghouse now!
That is just a drop in the bucket.
The doctor says I'm fit as a fiddle.

After winning the lottery, I'll be on Easy Street.
The storekeeper wanted cash on the barrelhead.
I broke the window, and I'm in hot water now!
He bought the company and then lost his shirt.
After the accident, things were touch and go.
You have to make hay while the sun shines.
What I say to him goes in one ear and out the other.
Don't make a mountain out of a molehill.
I'll keep my eye on the baby for you.
The dead fish smelled to high heaven.
I saw the snake and almost jumped out of my skin.
She surely goes hog wild getting a party ready.
We played a game at the party to break the ice.
To clean that dirty oven, I have to use lots of elbow grease.
He cried wolf one too many times.
Don't cry over spilt milk.
You're skating on thin ice when you tell your mother a lie.
Are you getting cold feet about asking for more money?
Many sailors have gone to Davy Jones's locker.
He got into the party by crashing the gate.
He's just trying to keep up with the Joneses.

47

TABLE OF CONTENTS

- Look for new words in every book you read. Practice pronouncing and writing them.

- Learn to spell one new word every day.

- Read catalog descriptions to find words used to influence consumers to buy catalog items. Use the words in some written form within three days.

- Pick a word.
  —Write rhyming words.
  —Use it to make new words.
  —List synonyms.
  —List antonyms.
  —List homonyms.
  —List heteronyms.
  —Write a paragraph about the word.
  —Look up the meaning in your dictionary.
  —Write it like it feels.
  —Use it as the basis for a collage.
  —Challenge a friend to spell it.

- Write a play you'd like for your class to present. Be sure to make the dialogue interesting, entertaining, and original.

- Play Scrabble, Word Bingo, Spell-O, and Boggle.

- Make regular deposits in your own word and phrase bank. Use these as starters, and add more of your own.

Linking Words: however	moreover	therefore	furthermore
hence	meanwhile	whereas	nevertheless

  Words That Show Time Order:

later	before	finally	earlier
first	then	next	afterward

- Make lists of words and phrases that:
  —Add pizzazz
  —Create excitement
  —Describe
  —Arouse curiosity
  —Demand attention
  —Build suspense

- Write to a pen pal, preferably one your own age who lives in another country. Use interesting and descriptive words and phrases to tell about yourself, your home, and your own particular interests.

IDEAS FOR EXPANDING A WRITING VOCABULARY

- Use a guide to free and inexpensive learning materials to find three sets of information materials you would like to have. Select materials on topics you know little or nothing about, and write letters requesting the materials. If you don't have a current, updated guide, you need one. A good one is:

  Free and Inexpensive Learning Materials by George Peabody College for Teachers. (Available from Incentive Publications, Inc., P.O. Box 120189, Nashville, TN 37212, at a cost of $4.50 plus $1.00 for shipping and handling charges.)

- Keep a diary—make it personal and private.

- Become a list-maker. Start with lists of:
  —Things to do
  —Wishes
  —TV and radio programs
  —Names and addresses
  —Important events
  —Places to go
  —Things to see
  —Budgets

- Design your own greeting cards complete with unique and original messages from you!

- Pick out and pronounce the rhyming words as you read poetry.

- Read cook books, game books, and other books giving directions in a sequential manner. Make a list of the words used frequently to tell the reader "what to do," "when to do," and "how to do."

- Make a list of twenty careers that interest you. Use your dictionary or thesaurus to find one or more unusual synonyms for each of the careers.

- Write a letter to your senator or representative about a matter of concern to you. Use ten words that you've never used in a letter before.

- Look in the Yellow Pages of the telephone book to find words frequently used in ads. Just for fun, make a list of all the three-syllable words that are used more than three times on one page.

- Daydream, and write down your dreams.

- Make a list of your friends and family members and their birthday. Send one of your original greeting cards to each one on the appropriate day.

- Hang a large piece of paper on a wall in your room. Each time you learn a new word, write it in fancy script on the paper. Use lots of different colors to make your "Word Wall" interesting and attractive.

THINGS TO WRITE ON

stationery, tablets, pads, notebooks
acetate
file folders
fabric
index cards
tissues
grocery sacks, shopping bags
gift bags
paper towels
kites
your hands and feet (or someone else's, with
    their permission)
bodies
gift-wrap paper
canvas
cardboard, posterboard, tagboard
construction paper
tissue paper
cakes
cookies
adding machine tape
old window shade
plastic tablecloth
hats
T-shirts
old lamp shades
paper plates and cups
wooden spoons
shirt boards
*bath tubs
*sinks
leaves, stones, and rocks
*shovels
*mirrors
*windows
toilet paper
wood strips, shingles
*cookie sheets
*pot lids
*sidewalks, streets
bricks and concrete blocks
*drinking glasses
*sunglasses
*dust pans (make good wings)
*plastic plates, cups, and glasses
*formica table tops
*glass table tops
*refrigerator doors
old wallpaper
fingers of a glove
boxes
* Be sure to use water-soluble writing
  materials on these!

THINGS TO WRITE WITH

pencil
pen
chalk
paint
soap
shoe polish
shaving cream
toothpaste
feather
lipstick
cake frosting
yarn or twine
glue
mud
twigs and sticks
paint brushes
sponges
ribbon
string
tape
finger and toes
shells
stones
syrup
pudding
salt
buttons
rope
beans
seeds
cereal
nails and tacks
rags and cotton balls
large-headed pins
blocks
letters cut from magazines, newspaper,
    bulletins, and brochures
paper punched holes
needle and thread
embroidery thread
dental floss
words cut from greeting cards
paper clips (glued together or laid end to end)
string beans
spaghetti
pretzel sticks
whipped cream
crayons
wet ashes
felt markers
press-on letters

The famous ballerina leaped into the air . . .
A huge black bear lumbered toward the highway . . .
Out of the darkness and into the campfire's light came . . .
Please don't say . . .
In magnificent splendor . . .
Suddenly, the sky lit up . . .
A piercing scream broke the stillness . . .
Silly, I know, but . . .
The excitement of the midway became contagious . . .
I don't believe in magic pencils, but . . .
The crocodile opened his jaws wide . . .
Senators should be careful about what they eat . . .
The train roared on into the night . . .
In a split second . . .
The unbelievably beautiful sunset . . .
The fog set in at midday . . .
Snips and snails and sand pails . . .
Miles and miles of forbidding coast line stretched ahead . . .
A house just as desolate as the one before . . .
Where the tornado hit . . .
I'm sorry, but that's just how it is . . .
A ghost walked here last night . . .
The boat slowly pulled away from the shore . . .
Man's best friend is . . .
Women's best friend is . . .
The drill captain roared . . .
As flood waters continued to rise . . .
Right in my own backyard, I . . .
The driver looked away for just a second . . .
A strange smell came from the swamp . . .
The whole horizon was covered by a dark cloud . . .
The stone simply would not budge . . .
I became more frightened with every step . . .
Under the giant mushroom . . .
The day the teacher overslept, we . . .
We played this crazy game in which you had to . . .
It all started when . . .
All the kids on the block waited anxiously . . .
The strangest looking dog I've ever seen . . .
The curtains in back of the dusty window parted slowly, and . . .
If I live to be one hundred and four, I'll never . . .
The last bar on the cage gave way, and the lion . . .
The flashlight was shining directly into my tent . . .
The ground began to sink down, down, down . . .
He's been missing for more than two days . . .
Suddenly, the lantern sputtered and went out . . .
A pocket knife is the only clue to . . .
More than anything in the world, she wanted to . . .
Gold!!! . . .
Under the pillow was a note saying . . .
Gigantic footprints led right up to the . . .
As the band began to play, . . .
Caught in the act again! . . .
Get me out of here, please . . .
The label said, "Open at your own risk." . . .
I felt my body shrinking, shrinking . . .
He stuck his hand in the opening, and pulled out . . .
The whole town was in an uproar . . .

5

When the little fish asked the leviathan, "Are you ill?" he replied, "No, I'm whale."
Did you hear about the smart pole vaulter who really had the jump on things?
A silly lady is a dumb belle.
A swimming animal that barks is a dog fish.
"Dash it all!" exclaimed the runner.
The ruling animal is the reign-deer.
An octopus is a cat with eight sides.
Said the scissors-happy film director, "Cut! Cut!"
When asked why he was being spanked, the confused child said, "Beats me!"
A lost puppy is a dog gone.
"Don't drop the eggs," cracked the grocer.
Did you hear about the snobbish robbery victim who was really stuck up?
"I love all people," said the cannibal.
If your refrigerator is running, you should try to catch it!
A well is a deep subject.
As the lawyer said, "Just in case."
Said the golfer as he searched for his lost ball, "I don't know where I putt it."
A kindergarten teacher tries to make little things count.
Said the grizzly, "I can't bear it any more."
"I always let things slide," said the trombonist.
The dentist said, "My occupation is very filling."
"Could you please hurry?" said the man on his way to the cleaners. "I have a pressing engagement."
My cookbook certainly is exciting—it contains such stirring events.
A teacher without students has no class.
The baker really got a rise out of that.
The largest ants in the world are gi-ants.
That butcher is really a cut above.
"See you around," said the circle.
When the salesman left, he said, "Buy, buy!"
The strangest creature I've ever seen is a spelling bee.
The author said, "Write on!"
A sign hanging on an old boat: "For sail."
The tailor said, "Will this outfit suit you, sir?"
A clockmaker always works overtime.
Another name for an angrily rising ocean is an emergent sea (emergency).
"I want no part of that," said the bald man.
A barber runs a clip joint.
"Hand it over," said the manicurist.
The shoemaker said, "That boot really has sole!"
The principal part of a lion is its mane.
The night watchman said, "I've never done a day's work."
Dawn breaks but never falls.
The astronomer said, "My business is looking up."
I thought that Dracula movie was a pain in the neck.
The farmer said, "Sow what?"
He could be a wonderful pianist except for two things—his hands.
A demon's favorite dessert is devil's food cake.
The seamstress said, "You're sew right!"
This horn isn't broken—it just doesn't give a hoot!
When the nuclear scientist went on vacation, he left a sign on his door that read, "Gone fission."
The surgeon said, "I'll keep you in stitches."
Did you hear about the clergyman who wanted to make a parson-to-parson call?
If you stuck your head in a washing machine, you'd get brainwashed.
Niagara Falls but never breaks.
Did you hear about the wolf that got trapped in the laundry and became a wash and werewolf?

6

YOUNG WRITER'S CHECK LIST

Things to Write About	Date	Comments
Adventure		
Art		
Bodies of Water		
Books		
Communication		
Current Events		
Daydreams		
Families		
Fantasies		
Feelings		
Folklore		
the Future		
Gardening and Farming		
Geography		
Ghosts, Goblins, Witches, Fairies, Elves, and Trolls		
History		
Hobbies		
Holidays		
Land Formations		
Long Ago		
Manners		
Money		
Music		
Politics		
Problems		
Propaganda		
Religion		
Scenery		
Science		
Seasons		
Social Events		
Someone Else's Life		
Sports		
a Town, City, or Country		
Tragedy		
Transportation		
Travel		
Trivia		
the Unknown		
the Weather		
Your Life		

Things to Write	Date	Comments
Ads		
Anecdotes		
Autobiographies		
Biographies		
Brochures		
Bulletins		
Cartoons		
Editorials		
Fables		
Feature Articles		
Graffiti		
Greeting Cards		
"How To" Booklets		
Jokes		
Letters		
Lists		
Minutes		
Myths		
Notes		
Novels		
Pamphlets		
Plays		
Poetry Forms		
Cinquains		
Couplets		
Free Verse		
Haiku		
Limericks		
Nursery Rhymes		
Odes		
Quatrains		
Sonnets		
Triplets		
Recipes		
Reports		
Riddles		
Science Fiction		
Slogans		
Songs		
Speeches		
Stories		
Tall Tales		

Feeling words
Sound words
Color words
Time words
Friendly words
Unfriendly words
Number words
City words
Country words
Day words
Night words
Home words
School words
Art words
Theater words
Food words
Ocean words
Valley words
Hill words
Jungle words
Mountain words
Desert words
Seashore words
Shopping words
Appreciation words
Disappointment words
Sad words
Glad words
Clothing words
Fashion words
Suspense words
Fat words
Thin words

Holiday words
Hate words
Adventure words
Store words
Family words
Religious words
Taste words
Love words
Hot words
Cold words
Circus words
Goodbye words
Hello words
Airplane words
Train words
Truck words
Automobile words
Swimming words
Football words
Golf words
Space words
Advertising words
Tennis words
Baseball words
Basketball words
Scratchy words
Yes words
No words

Election words
Size words
Shape words
War words
Peace words
Nonsense words
Season words
Weather words
Radio words
Newspaper words
TV words
Career words
Baby words
Children words
Teen-age words
Adult words
Teacher words
Pizzazz words
Nature words
Music words
Feminine words
Masculine words
Library words
Tax words
Mineral words
Plant words
Animal words
Hotel words
Restaurant words
Health words
Gym words
Excitement words
Fear words

Start your own "Big Book of Word Lists,"
and see how long it takes you to add 100 or
more categories with at least five words in
each category!

ability (power), **capacity** (condition)

accede (agree), **exceed** (surpass)

accept (receive), **except** (exclude)

adapt (adjust), **adopt** (accept)

advise (to give advice), **advice** (counsel or recommendation)

affect (to influence), **effect** (result)

all ready (completely prepared), **already** (previously)

allude (to refer to), **elude** (escape)

allusion (reference), **illusion** (false perception), **delusion** (false belief)

assure (to set a person's mind at ease), **insure** (guarantee life or property against harm), **ensure** (to secure from harm)

avenge (to achieve justice), **revenge** (retaliation)

averse (opposition on the subject's part), **adverse** (opposition against the subject's will)

avoid (shun), **prevent** (thwart), **avert** (turn away)

between (use when referring to two persons, places or things), **among** (use when referring to more than two places, persons, or things)

capital (seat of government), **capitol** (building)

censor (one who prohibits offensive material), **censure** (to criticize)

cite (to bring forward as support or truth), **quote** (to repeat exactly)

clench (to grip something tightly, as hand or teeth), **clinch** (to secure a bargain or something abstract)

complement (something that completes), **compliment** (an expression of praise)

compromise (a settlement in which each side makes concession), **surrender** (to yield completely)

confidant (one to whom secrets are told), **confidante** (a female confidant), **confident** (assured of success)

constant (unchanging), **continual** (repeated regularly), **continuous** (action without interruption)

contagious (transmissable by contact), **infectious** (capable of causing infection)

consul (a country's representative in a foreign country), **council** (a deliberative assembly), **councilor** (member of a deliberative body), **counsel** (to give advice), **counselor** (one who gives advice)

credible (plausible), **creditable** (deserving commendation), **credulous** (gullible)

deny (contradict), **refute** (to give evidence to disprove something), **repudiate** (to reject the validity of)

doubtless (presumption of certainty), **undoubtedly** (definite certainty)

elegy (a mournful poem), **eulogy** (a speech honoring a deceased person)

element (a basic assumption), **factor** (something that contributes to a result)

elicit (to evoke), **illicit** (unlawful)

emigrate (a single move by persons, used with *from*), **immigrate** (a single move by persons, used with *to*), **migrate** (seasonal movement)

eminent (prominent), **imminent** (soon to occur)

farther (literal distance), **further** (figurative distance)

fatal (causing death), **fateful** (affecting one's destiny)

feasible (clearly possible), **possible** (capable of happening)

fewer (refers to units capable of being individually counted), **less** (refers to collective quantities or to abstracts)

graceful (refers to movement), **gracious** (courteous)

impassable (impossible to traverse), **impassive** (devoid of emotion)

imply (to hint or suggest), **infer** (to draw conclusions based on facts)

incredible (unbelievable), **incredulous** (skeptical)

insignificant (trivial), **tiny** (small)

insinuate (to hint covertly), **intimate** (to imply subtly)

invoke (to call upon a higher power for assistance), **evoke** (to reawaken or inspire)

judical (pertaining to law), **judicious** (exhibiting sound judgment)

latter (the second of two things mentioned), **later** (subsequently)

lay (to put or place), **lie** (to recline)

10

likely (use when mere probability is involved), **apt** (use when a known tendency is involved)

mania (craze), **phobia** (fear)

may (use when strong sense of permission or possibility is involved), **might** (use when weak sense of permission or possibility is involved)

mutual (refers to intangibles of a personal nature between two parties), **reciprocal** (refers to a balanced relationship in which one action is made on account of or in return for another)

nauseated (to feel queasy), **nauseous** (causing queasiness)

oblige (to feel a debt of gratitude), **obligate** (under direct compulsion to follow a certain course)

official (authorized by a proper authority), **officious** (extremely eager to offer help or advice)

older (refers to persons and things), **elder** (refers only to persons)

on (used to indicate motion to a position), **onto** (very strongly conveys motion toward) **on to** (use when *on* is an adverb and *to* is a preposition)

oral (refers to the sense of "word of mouth;" cannot refer to written words), **verbal** (can refer to both written and spoken words)

partly (use when stress is placed on a part in contrast to the whole), **partially** (use when the whole is stressed, often indirectly)

people (refers to a large group of individuals considered collectively), **persons** (refers to a small, specific number), **public** (a group of people sharing a common interest)

persecute (to oppress or harass), **prosecute** (to initiate legal or criminal action against)

piteous (pathetic), **pitiable** (lamentable), **pitiful** (very inferior or insignificant)

practically (almost), **virtually** (to all intents)

precipitant (rash, impulsive), **precipitate** (to hurl downward), **precipitous** (extremely steep)

principal (chief), **principle** (basic law or truth)

quite (very), **quiet** (hushed)

rack (a framework; to be in great pain), **wrack** (destruction by violent means)

raise (to move upward; to build; to breed), **rear** (to bring up a child), **rise** (to ascend)

rare (refers to unusual value and quality of which there is a permanent small supply), **scarce** (refers to temporary infrequency)

ravage (to devastate or despoil), **ravish** (to take away by force; to rape)

recourse (an application to something for aid or support), **resource** (an available supply)

regretful (sorrowful), **regrettable** (something that elicits mental distress)

reluctant (unwilling), **reticent** (refers to a temperament or style that is characteristically silent or restrained)

repel (drive off; cause distaste or aversion), **repulse** (drive off; reject by means of discourtesy)

respectfully (showing honor and esteem), **respectively** (one at a time in order)

restive (resistance to control), **restless** (lacking repose)

seasonal (refers to what applies to or depends on a season), **seasonable** (refers to timeliness or appropriateness to a season)

sensual (used when referring to the gratification of physical [sexual] senses), **sensuous** (usually refers to senses involved in aesthetic gratification)

sit (to rest the body on the buttocks with the torso upright; usually intransitive), **set** (to put or place something; usually transitive)

specific (explicitly set forth), **particular** (not general or universal)

stationary (immovable), **stationery** (matched writing paper and envelopes)

tasteful (exhibiting that which is proper or seemly in a social setting), **tasty** (having a pleasing flavor)

transient (refers to what literally stays for only a short time), **transitory** (sort-lived, impermanent)

turbid (muddy, dense; in turmoil), **turgid** (swollen; grandiloquent)

The following spelling rules are generalizations, and do not work all of the time. However, they are often true, and are valuable spelling aids.

1. Each syllable of a word must contain one sounded vowel. (al li ga tor)

2. A vowel is more likely to be pronounced short than long.

3. A vowel at the end of a one-syllable word is usually long. (be)

4. The final e in a one-syllable word is usually silent. (lake)

5. When i precedes gh, it is usually long. (bright)

6. I comes before e except after c , or when sounded like a as in neighbor, and weigh. (chief, receive)

7. Usually, a doubled consonant or vowel has one sound. (letter, boot)

8. When two vowels are together, the first one usually says its own name. (team)

9. The ch shound is often spelled tch. (catch)

10. The j sound is often spelled dg or dge. (dredging, smudge)

11. The k sound may be made by c or ck. (came, stack)

12. The gh combination is usually silent (dough, fright,) but sometimes it sounds like f (trough, laugh).

13. The consonants c and h are soft before i, e, and y; otherwise, they are hard. (go, gentle; center, car)

14. The ending -ance may also be spelled -ence. (endurance, presence)

15. The ending -ous may be used with an e or an i. (ominous, extraneous, delicious)

16. The ending -tion may be spelled -cian, -sian, -sion, or -tian. (station, physician, Prussian, decision, Dalmatian)

17. Pluralize a word that ends in y with a consonant before it by changing the y to i and adding es. (cry, cries)

18. The common prefixes en-, in-, and un- are not used interchangeably.

Amazing—incredible, unbelievable, improbable, fabulous, wonderful, fantastic, astonishing, astounding, extraordinary

Anger—enrage, infuriate, arouse, nettle, exasperate, inflame, madden

Angry—mad, furious, enraged, excited, wrathful, indignant, exasperated, aroused, inflamed

Answer—reply, respond, retort, acknowledge

Ask—question, inquire of, seek information from, put a question to, demand, request, expect, inquire, query, interrogate, examine, quiz

Awful—dreadful, terrible, abominable, bad, poor, unpleasant

Bad—evil, immoral, wicked, corrupt, sinful, depraved, rotten, contaminated, spoiled, tainted, harmful, injurious, unfavorable, defective, inferior, imperfect, substandard, faulty, improper, inappropriate, unsuitable, disagreeable, unpleasant, cross, nasty, unfriendly, irascible, horrible, atrocious, outrageous, scandalous, infamous, wrong, noxious, sinister, putrid, snide, deplorable, dismal, gross, heinous, nefarious, base, obnoxious, detestable, despicable, contemptible, foul, rank, ghastly, execrable

Beautiful—pretty, lovely, handsome, attractive, gorgeous, dazzling, splendid, magnificent, comely, fair, ravishing, graceful, elegant, fine, exquisite, aesthetic, pleasing, shapely, delicate, stunning, glorious, heavenly, resplendent, radiant, glowing, blooming, sparkling

Begin—start, open, launch, initiate, commence, inaugurate, originate

Big—enormous, huge, immense, gigantic, vast, colossal, gargantuan, large, sizeable, grand, great, tall, substantial, mammoth, astronomical, ample, broad, expansive, spacious, stout, tremendous, titanic, mountainous

Brave—courageous, fearless, dauntless, intrepid, plucky, daring, heroic, valorous, audacious, bold, gallant, valiant, doughty, mettlesome, plucky

Break—fracture, rupture, shatter, smash, wreck, crash, demolish, atomize

Bright—shining, shiny, gleaming, brilliant, sparkling, shimmering, radiant, vivid, colorful, lustrous, luminous, incandescent, intelligent, brilliant, knowing, quick-witted, smart, intellectual

Calm—quiet, peaceful, still, tranquil, mild, serene, smooth, composed, collected, unruffled, level-headed, unexcited, detached, aloof

Come—approach, advance, near, arrive, reach

Cool—chilly, cold, frosty, wintry, icy, frigid

Crooked—bent, twisted, curved, hooked, zigzag

Cry—shout, yell, yowl, scream, roar, bellow, weep, wail, sob, bawl

Cut—gash, slash, prick, nick, sever, slice, carve, cleave, slit, chop, crop, lop, reduce

Dangerous—perilous, hazardous, risky, uncertain, unsafe

Dark—shadowy, unlit, murky, gloomy, dim, dusky, shaded, sunless, black, dismal, sad, gloomy

Decide—determine, settle, choose, resolve

Definite—certain, sure, positive, determined, clear, distinct, obvious

Delicious—savory, delectable, appetizing, luscious, scrumptious, palatable, delightful, enjoyable, toothsome, exquisite

Describe—portray, characterize, picture, narrate, relate, recount, represent, report, record

Destroy—ruin, demolish, raze, waste, kill, slay, end, extinguish

Difference—disagreement, inequality, contrast, dissimilarity, incompatibility

Do—execute, enact, carry out, finish, conclude, effect, accomplish, achieve, attain

Dull—boring, tiring, tiresome, uninteresting, slow, dumb, stupid, unimaginative, lifeless, dead, insensible, tedious, wearisome, listless, expressionless, plain, monotonous, humdrum, dreary

Eager—keen, fervent, enthusiastic, involved, interested, alive to

End—stop, finish, terminate, conclude, close, halt, cessation, discontinuance

Enjoy—appreciate, delight in, be pleased, indulge in, luxuriate in, bask in, relish, devour, savor, like

Explain—elaborate, clarify, define, interpret, justify, account for

Fair—just, impartial, unbiased, objective, unprejudiced, honest

Fall—drop, descend, plunge, topple, tumble

False—fake, fraudulent, counterfeit, spurious, untrue, unfounded, erroneous, deceptive, groundless, fallacious

Famous—well-known, renowned, celebrated, famed, eminent, illustrious, distinguished, noted, notorious

Fast—quick, rapid, swift, speedy, fleet, hasty, snappy, mercurial, swiftly, rapidly, quickly, snappily, speedily, lickety-split, posthaste, hastily, expeditiously, like a flash

Fat—stout, corpulent, fleshy, beefy, paunchy, plump, full, rotund, tubby, pudgy, chubby, chunky, burly, bulky, hippopotamic, elphantine

Fear—fright, dread, terror, alarm, dismay, anxiety, scare, awe, horror, panic, apprehension

Fly—soar, hover, flit, wing, flee, waft, glide, coast, skim, sail, cruise

Funny—humorous, amusing, droll, comic, comical, laughable, silly

Get—acquire, obtain, secure, procure, gain, fetch, find, score, accumulate, win, earn, reap, catch, net, bag, derive, collect, gather, glean, pick up, accept, come by, regain, salvage

Go—recede, depart, fade, disappear, move, travel, proceed

Good—excellent, fine, superior, wonderful, marvelous, qualified, suited, suitable, apt, proper, capable, generous, kindly, friendly, gracious, obliging, pleasant, agreeable, pleasurable, satisfactory, well-behaved, obedient, honorable, reliable, trustworthy, safe, favorable, profitable, advantageous, righteous, expedient, helpful, valid, genuine, ample, salubrious, estimable, beneficial, splendid, great, noble, worthy, first-rate, top-notch, grand, sterling, superb, respectable, edifying

Great—noteworthy, worthy, distinguished, remarkable, grand, considerable, powerful, much, mighty

Gross—improper, rude, coarse, indecent, crude, vulgar, outrageous, extreme, grievous, shameful, uncouth, obscene, low

Happy—pleased, contented, satisfied, delighted, elated, joyful, cheerful, ecstatic, jubilant, gay, tickled, gratified, glad, blissful, overjoyed

Hate—depise, loathe, detest, abhor, disfavor, dislike, disapprove, abominate

Have—hold, possess, own, contain, acquire, gain, maintain, believe, bear, beget, occupy, absorb, fill, enjoy

Help—aid, assist, support, encourage, back, wait on, attend, serve, relieve, succor, benefit, befriend, abet

Hide—conceal, cover, mask, cloak, camouflage, screen, shroud, veil

Hurry—rush, run, speed, race, hasten, urge, accelerate, bustle

Hurt—damage, harm, injure, wound, distress, afflict, pain

Idea—thought, concept, conception, notion, understanding, opinion, plan, view, belief

SYNONYMS FOR WORDS COMMONLY USED IN CHILDREN'S WRITINGS

Important—necessary, vital, critical, indispensable, valuable, essential, significant, primary, principal, considerable, famous, distinguished, notable, well-known

Interesting—fascinating, engaging, sharp, keen, bright, intelligent, animated, spirited, attractive, inviting, intriguing, provocative, thought-provoking, challenging, inspiring, involving, moving, titillating, tantalizing, exciting, entertaining, piquant, lively, racy, spicy, engrossing, absorbing, consuming, gripping, arresting, enthralling, spellbinding, curious, captivating, enchanting, bewitching, appealing,

Keep—hold, retain, withhold, preserve, maintain, sustain, support

Kill—slay, execute, assassinate, murder, destroy, cancel, abolish

Lazy—indolent, slothful, idle, inactive, sluggish

Little—tiny, small, diminutive, shrimp, runt, miniature, puny, exiguous, dinky, cramped, limited, itsy-bitsy, microscopic, slight, petite, minute

Look—gaze, see, glance, watch, survey, study, seek, search for, peek, peep, glimpse, stare, contemplate, examine, gape, ogle, scrutinize, inspect, leer, behold, observe, view, witness, perceive, spy, sight, discover, notice, recognize, peer, eye, gawk, peruse, explore

Love—like, admire, esteem, fancy, care for, cherish, adore, treasure, worship, appreciate, savor

Make—create, originate, invent, beget, form, construct, design, fabricate, manufacture, produce, build, develop, do, effect, execute, compose, perform, accomplish, earn, gain, obtain, acquire, get

Mark—label, tag, price, ticket, impress, effect, trace, imprint, stamp, brand, sign, note, heed, notice, designate

Mischievous—prankish, playful, naughty, roguish, waggish, impish, sportive

Move—plod, go, creep, crawl, inch, poke, drag, toddle, shuffle, trot, dawdle, walk, traipse, mosey, jog, plug, trudge, stump, lumber, trail, lag, run, sprint, trip, bound, hotfoot, high-tail, streak, stride, tear, breeze, whisk, rush, dash, dart, bolt, fling, scamper, scurry, skedaddle, scoot, scuttle, scramble, race, chase, hasten, hurry, hump, gallop, lope, accelerate, stir, budge, travel, wander, roam, journey, trek, ride, spin, slip, glide, slide, slither, coast, flow, sail, saunter, hobble, amble, stagger, paddle, slouch, prance, straggle, meander, perambulate, waddle, wobble, pace, swagger, promenade, lunge

Moody—temperamental, changeable, short-tempered, glum, morose, sullen, mopish, irritable, testy, peevish, fretful, spiteful, sulky, touchy

Neat—clean, orderly, tidy, trim, dapper, natty, smart, elegant, well-organized, super, desirable, spruce, shipshape, well-kept, shapely

New—fresh, unique, original, unusual, novel, modern, current, recent

Old—feeble, frail, ancient, weak, aged, used, worn, dilapidated, ragged, faded, broken-down, former, old-fashioned, outmoded, passe, veteran, mature, venerable, primitive, traditional, archaic, conventional, customary, stale, musty, obsolete, extinct

Part—portion, share, piece, allotment, section, fraction, fragment

Place—space, area, spot, plot, region, location, situation, position, residence, dwelling, set, site, station, status, state

Plan—plot, scheme, design, draw, map, diagram, procedure, arrangement, intention, device, contrivance, method, way, blueprint

Popular—well-liked, approved, accepted, favorite, celebrated, common, current

Predicament—quandary, dilemma, pickle, problem, plight, spot, scrape, jam

Put—place, set, attach, establish, assign, keep, save, set aside, effect, achieve, do, build

Quiet—silent, still, soundless, mute, tranquil, peaceful, calm, restful

Right—correct, accurate, factual, true, good, just, honest, upright, lawful, moral, proper, suitable, apt, legal, fair

Run—race, speed, hurry, hasten, sprint, dash, rush, escape, elope, flee

Say/Tell—inform, notify, advise, relate, recount, narrate, explain, reveal, disclose, divulge, declare, command, order, bid, enlighten, instruct, insist, teach, train,, direct, issue, remark, converse, speak, affirm, suppose, utter, negate, express, verbalize, voice, articulate, pronounce, deliver, convey, impart, assert, state, allege, mutter, mumble, whisper, sigh, exclaim, yell, sing, yelp, snarl, hiss, grunt, snort, roar, bellow, thunder, boom, scream, shriek, screech, squawk, whine, philosophize, stammer, stutter, lisp, drawl, jabber, protest, announce, swear, vow, contend, assure, deny dispute

Scared—afraid, frightened, alarmed, terrified, panicked, fearful, unnerved, insecure, timid, shy, skittish, jumpy, disquieted, worried, vexed, troubled, disturbed, horrified, terrorized, shocked, petrified, haunted, timorous, shrinking, tremulous, stupefied, paralyzed, stunned, apprehensive

Show—display, exhibit, present, note, point to, indicate, explain, reveal, prove, demonstrate, expose

Slow—unhurried, gradual, leisurely, late, behind, tedious, slack

Stop—cease, halt, stay, pause, discontinue, conclude, end, finish, quit

Story—tale, myth, legend, fable, yarn, account, narrative, chronicle, epic, sage, anecdote, record, memoir

Strange—odd, peculiar, unusual, unfamiliar, uncommon, queer, wierd, outlandish, curious, unique, exclusive, irregular

Take—hold, catch, seize, grasp, win, capture, acquire, pick, choose, select, prefer, remove, steal, lift, rob, engage, bewitch, purchase, buy, retract, recall, assume, occupy, consume

Tell—disclose, reveal, show, expose, uncover, relate, narrate, inform, advise, explain, divulge, declare, command, order, bid, recount, repeat

Think—judge, deem, assume, believe, consider, contemplate, reflect, meditate

Trouble—distress, anguish, anxiety, worry, wretchedness, pain, danger, peril, disaster, grief, misfortune, difficulty, concern, pains, inconvenience, exertion, effort

True—accurate, right, proper, precise, exact, valid, genuine, real, actual, trusty, steady, loyal, dependable, sincere, staunch

Ugly—hideous, frightful, frightening, shocking, horrible, unpleasant, monstrous, terrifying, gross, grisly, ghastly, horrid, unsightly, plain, homely, evil, repulsive, repugnant, gruesome

Unhappy—miserable, uncomfortable, wretched, heart-broken, unfortunate, poor,, downhearted, sorrowful, depressed, dejected, melancholy, glum, gloomy, dismal, discouraged, sad

Use—employ, utilize, exhaust, spend, expend, consume, exercise

Wrong—incorrect, inaccurate, mistaken, erroneous, improper, unsuitable

wish	**dream**	**boy**	**girl**	**match**	**love**	**miss**
dish	cream	ahoy	curl	batch	above	bliss
fish	gleam	coy	hurl	catch	dove	hiss
squish	seam	enjoy	pearl	hatch	glove	kiss
swish	team	joy	swirl	latch	of	sis
	steam	toy	twirl	patch	shove	this

cat	**bunk**	**ball**	**weak**	**think**	**rain**
bat	clunk	call	beak	blink	cane
fat	dunk	crawl	cheek	brink	gain
flat	drunk	fall	leak	clink	lain
hat	hunk	gall	meek	drink	main
mat	junk	hall	peak	link	pain
pat	punk	mall	peek	pink	rain
rat	sunk	stall	reek	rink	stain
sat	stunk	tall	seek	sink	train
slat	trunk	wall	week	wink	vain

and	**bare**	**black**	**block**	**blue**	**date**
band	bear	back	clock	clue	ate
brand	care	crack	cock	crew	bait
canned	dare	lack	dock	drew	fate
fanned	fare	pack	flock	few	gate
gland	hair	quack	knock	flew	hate
grand	pear	rack	lock	glue	late
hand	rare	sack	mock	knew	mate
land	stare	smack	rock	new	rate
sand	there	stack	sock	to	state
stand	wear	track	tock	true	wait

day	**dear**	**eye**	**four**	**friend**	**gold**
clay	deer	by	core	bend	bold
gay	fear	cry	door	blend	bowled
hay	hear	fry	floor	end	cold
lay	here	I	more	lend	fold
may	near	high	pour	mend	hold
play	peer	lie	roar	pretend	mold
ray	queer	pie	sore	rend	old
say	rear	sigh	store	send	rolled
tray	steer	tie	tore	spend	sold
way	year	why	wore	tend	told

RHYMING WORDS

book	burn	time	fist	five	six	ten
brook	churn	crime	grist	chive	fix	been
cook	earn	dime	hissed	dive	kicks	den
crook	fern	grime	kissed	drive	licks	hen
hook	learn	lime	list	hive	picks	men
look	stern	rhyme	mist	jive	sticks	pen
rook	turn	slime	twist	live	ticks	when
took	yearn				wicks	yen

dog	thought	star	tin	bowl	man
cog	bought	are	bin	coal	ban
fog	brought	bar	din	foal	can
flog	caught	car	fin	goal	fan
frog	fought	far	gin	hole	pan
hog	ought	jar	kin	mole	plan
jog	sought	mar	pin	pole	ran
log	taught	tar	sin	roll	tan
smog	taut	war	win	soul	van

grade	green	map	night	nine	ring
ade	bean	cap	bite	dine	bring
blade	clean	clap	bright	fine	cling
fade	dean	flap	fight	line	ding
glade	glean	gap	kite	mine	fling
laid	keen	lap	light	pine	king
made	lean	nap	quite	sign	sing
maid	mean	slap	right	swine	sling
paid	queen	tap	sight	tine	sting
raid	seen	trap	tight	vine	swing
wade	teen	wrap	white	whine	wing

room	run	tale	three	tone	snow
boom	bun	dale	be	bone	blow
bloom	done	fail	flea	cone	crow
broom	fun	gale	glee	groan	flow
doom	gun	hale	key	known	go
gloom	none	jail	knee	lone	know
groom	one	male	me	moan	low
loom	pun	nail	see	phone	mow
room	sun	pale	tea	stone	no
tomb	ton	rail	tree	thrown	row
zoom	won	sale	we	zone	so

18

A **period** is used:
1. At the end of a declarative sentence.
2. At the end of an imperative sentence.
3. After numerals and letters in outlines.
4. At the end of a business request stated in question form.
5. After an abbreviation or an initial.

A **question mark** is used:
1. At the end of an interrogative sentence.
2. Inside parentheses after a date or statement to show doubt.

An **exclamation point** is used:
1. At the end of an exclamatory sentence.
2. After a very strong interjection.
3. At the end of an imperative sentence that exclaims.

A **comma** is used:
1. To separate items in a series.
2. To separate adjectives of equal value.
3. To separate a direct quotation from the rest of a sentence.
4. To separate the day of the month from the year.
5. To separate the names of a city and a state.
6. To separate a name from a title (David Bird, President)
7. To set off adjectives in an appositive position.
8. To set off introductory words like *no* and *now.*
9. To set off words like *however, moreover, too.*
10. To set off a name used in direct address.
11. To set off a nonrestrictive adjective clause.
12. To set off most words used in apposition.
13. After the greeting in a friendly letter.
14. After the closing in any letter.
15. After a last name preceding a first name.
16. After a mild interjection within a sentence.
17. After an introductory adverbial clause.
18. After an introductory participial phrase.
19. Before the conjunction in a compound sentence.
20. Whenever necessary to make meaning clear.

An **apostrophe** is used:
1. To show possession.
2. In contractions.
3. To form plurals of letters, figures, signs, and words.

Quotation marks are used:
1. To enclose the exact words of a speaker.
2. Around titles of short plays, short stories, short poems, chapter titles, and songs.

A **colon** is used:
1. In writing time (6:45).
2. To introduce a list.
3. After the greeting in a business letter.
4. In written plays and in other forms of written dialogue, after the name of the character who is speaking.

A **semicolon** is used:
1. To join independent clauses in a compound sentence when a conjunction is not present.
2. To precede a conjunctive adverb (therefore, however, furthermore, etc.) used between the coordinate clauses of a compound sentence.
3. In place of a comma when a more distinct pause than a comma indicates is desired.

Underlining is used:
1. Below handwritten or typewritten titles of movies, newspapers, books, magazines, ships, and trains.
2. To set off foreign words and phrases which are not yet part of the English language.

A **hyphen** is used:
1. In writing compound numbers.
2. To divide a word at the end of a line.
3. Between parts of a compound adjective preceding a noun.

A **dash** is used:
1. To indicate an abrubt break in thought or structure.
2. To indicate a parenthetical or explanatory phrase or clause.
3. Between numbers in a page reference.

Parentheses are used:
1. To enclose material that is supplementary, explanatory, or interpretive.
2. To enclose a question mark after a date or a statement to show doubt.
3. To enclose an author's insertion or comment.

Capitalize the first letter in:

1. The first word of a sentence.
2. The first word in each line of poetry.
3. The first and all other important words in the greeting of a letter.
4. The first word in the closing of a letter.
5. The first, last, and other main words in titles of chapters, stories, poems, reports, songs, books, movies, and radio and television programs.
6. The word I.
7. A proper adjective.
8. Initials.
9. Titles of persons (Mr., Ms., Mrs., Dr.).
10. Abbreviations (P.O., R.R., C.O.D., Dr.).
11. Titles of high government officials.
12. A proper noun.
13. Words like Mother, Sister, Uncle when used in place of or with names.
14. Names of schools, clubs, organizations, and buildings.
15. Names of streets, avenues, boulevards, roads, and Rural Route.
16. Names of cities, towns, counties, states, countries, and continents.
17. Names of rivers, oceans, mountains, and regions (the South).
18. Names of days, months, holidays, and other special days.
19. Names of businesses and special products.
20. Names of languages, nationalities, and special groups.
21. Names of political parties.
22. Names of government departments.
23. Names for the Deity.
24. Names of churches and religious denominations.
25. Names of historical events and documents.
26. Names of airlines, ships, and railroads.
27. Names of magazines and newspapers.
28. The first word of a head and a subhead in outlines.
29. The first word after a strong interjection.

BLOCK STYLE

(your street address)   *
(your city, state, and Zip)   *   Heading
(the date)

(addressee's name)
(company's name)   Inside Address
(company's street address)
(company's city, state, and Zip)

_____ :   Greeting/Salutation

_____
_____
_____
_____   Body of Letter
_____
_____
_____

_____ .   Complimentary Close

(your handwritten name)   Signature
(your typed name)

* Do not include if you are using paper with a letterhead on it.

MODIFIED BLOCK

Heading
                              (your street address)   *
                              (your city, state, and Zip) *
                              (the date)

(addressee's name)
(company's name)   Inside Address
(company's street address)
(company's city, state, and Zip)

_____ :   Greeting/Salutation

_____
_____
_____   Body of Letter
_____
_____
_____

Complimentary Close   _____ .

Signature   (your handwritten name)
                           (your typed name)

* Do not include if you are using paper with a letterhead on it.

MODIFIED SEMIBLOCK

Heading
                              (your street address)   *
                              (your city, state, and Zip) *
                              (the date)

(addressee's name)
(company's name)   Inside Address
(company's street address)
(company's city, state, and Zip)

_____ :   Greeting/Salutation

_____
_____
_____
_____   Body of Letter
_____
_____
_____

Complimentary Close   _____ .

Signature   (your handwritten name)
                           (your typed name)

* Do not include if you are using paper with a letterhead on it.

FRIENDLY LETTER

Heading
                              (your street address)   *
                              (your city, state, and Zip) *
                              (the date)

_____ ,   Greeting/Salutation

_____
_____   Body of Letter
_____
_____
_____
_____
_____
_____
_____

Complimentary Close   _____ .

Signature   _____

* Do not include if this information is printed or engraved on your stationery.

A A B B C C D D E E

F F G G H H I I J J

K K L L M M N N O O

P P Q Q R R S S T T

U U V V W W X X Y Y

Z Z a a b b c c d d e e

f f g g h h i i j j k k l l

m m n n o o p p q q r r s s

t t u u v v w w x x y y z z

1. Who will read my work?
2. Will they find it interesting?
3. Have I spelled all words correctly?
   (Check words you aren't sure about. Ask a good speller to read and check your spelling for you.)
4. Have I put periods, commas, question marks, quotation marks, exclamation points, and capital letters in the right places?
   (Reread to check yourself; then, ask a friend to double-check for you.)
5. Are my ideas in the right order?
   (Did I tell the first thing first and the others in sequence as they happened?)
6. Have I used words that my readers can understand easily?
7. Have I used interesting words that the reader will enjoy?
8. Have I used some examples or illustrations to help explain my ideas?
9. Have I said what I really think, and not just what I think my friends or my teacher would expect me to say?
10. Is my ending good? Does it really end the story or idea?
11. What is special about my writing that will make my readers be glad that they read it?

INTERMEDIATE EDITOR'S GUIDE

1. Have I visualized my reader? Do I understand what interests him?
2. Have I given careful attention to grammar, spelling, and punctuation so that my reader will experience no confusion in getting my message?
   (Proofread your writing, and then have a person skilled in proofreading recheck for technical errors.)
3. Have I expressed my thoughts in logical, sequential order?
   (Number the main ideas to check this.)
4. Have I used plain, simple words that are comfortable for my reader to read?
5. Have I used those plain, simple words in a way that will interest my reader?
6. Have I deleted unnecessary words and phrases?
   (Circle any word that could be left out and not change the meaning.)
7. Have I deleted unrelated or irrelevant matter?
   (Underline sentences or phrases that may not relate.)
8. Have I avoided overworked words, phrases, and clichés?
   (Cross out any you have used, and write a better synonym above each.)
9. Have I used the most active and "alive" words possible to express my ideas?
   (Look at each adjective and adverb. Ask yourself if there is a better, more interesting, more picturesque, or more precise word you might substitute.)
10. Have I used illustrations or examples to expand or reinforce main ideas?
    (Make an X at places where such entries may be helpful.)
11. Have I created added interest by interspersing figures of speech, forceful repetition, or exclamations into ordinary declarative thought?
    (Count the number of question marks, exclamation points, quotation marks, and figures of speech you have used.)
12. Have I expressed what I honestly feel or believe, or have I been more concerned about what my teacher or my peers will think?
    (Use tact and sensitivity in expressing negative or unpopular feelings or ideas, but do not sacrifice clarity or effectiveness.)
13. Have I referred to the beginning in the ending, and left my reader with an idea to ponder?
    (Will the reader feel that the article has been concluded thoughtfully? Have you said anything that will cause him to reconsider the subject?)

PROOFREADERS' MARKS

Instruction	Mark in Margin	Mark in Type	Corrected Type
Delete	ℰ	the ~~good~~ word	the word
Insert indicated material	good	the word	the good word
Let it stand	stet	the ~~good~~ word	the good word
Make capital	cap	the word	the Word
Make lower case	lc	The Word	the Word
Set in small capitals	sc	See word.	See WORD.
Set in italic type	ital	The word is word.	The word is *word*.
Set in roman type	rom	the (word)	the word
Set in boldface type	bf	the entry word	the entry **word**
Set in lightface type	lf	the entry (word)	the entry word
Transpose	tr	the word good	the good word
Close up space	◡	the wo rd	the word
Delete and close up space	ℰ̄	the wooord	the word
Spell out	sp	2 words	two words
Insert: space	#	theword	the word
period	⊙	This is the word	This is the word.
comma	⌄	words words, words	words, words, words
hyphen	^=^/^=^	word for word test	word-for-word test
colon	⊙	The following words	The following words:
semicolon	⌄	Scan the words skim the words.	Scan the words; skim the words.
apostrophe	⌄	Johns words	John's words
quotation marks	⌄/⌄/	the word word	the word "word"
parentheses	(/)/	The word word is in parentheses.	The word (word) is in parentheses.
brackets	[/]/	He read from the Word the Bible.	He read from the Word [the Bible].
en dash	⅟N	1964 1972	1964–1972
em dash	⅟M/⅟M/	The dictionary how often it is needed belongs in every home.	The dictionary—how often it is needed—belongs in every home.
superior type	⌄	$2 = 4$	$2^2 = 4$
inferior type	⌃	HO	H_2O
asterisk	⌄	word	word*
dagger	†	a word	a word†
double dagger	‡	words and words	words and words‡
section symbol	§	Book Reviews	§Book Reviews
virgule	/	either or	either/or
Start paragraph	¶	"Where is it?" "It's on the shelf."	"Where is it?" "It's on the shelf."
Run in	run in	The entry word is printed in boldface. The pronunciation follows.	The entry word is printed in boldface. The pronunciation follows.
Turn right side up	ꝺ	the word	the word
Move left	⊏	⊏ the word	the word
Move right	⊐	the word	the word
Move up	⊓	the word	the word
Move down	⊔	the word	the word
Align	‖	the word the word the word	the word the word the word
Straighten line	=	the word	the word
Wrong font	wf	the word	the word
Broken type	✕	the word	the word

Abstract Noun—a noun that names things which do not have a physical substance.
Example: *compassion.*

Active Voice—a verb which expresses action and can take a direct object.
Example: I *threw* the ball.

Adjective—a word that modifies a noun or a pronoun.
Example: the *white* ball.

Adverb—a word that modifies a verb, an adjective, or another adverb.
Example: Go *slowly.*

Antecendent—the word, phrase, or clause to which a relative pronoun refers. A pronoun must agree with its antecendent in number.
Example: *Erin* gave me his ball.

Articles—the adjectives *a, an,* and *the.*

Auxiliary Verb—a verb that accompanies another verb to show tense, mood, or voice.
Example: She *has* gone.

Clause—a group of words that contains a subject and a predicate, and forms part of a compound or complex sentence.
Example: *After I left, she called.*

Collective Noun—a noun that denotes a collection of persons or things regarded as a unit; usually takes a singular verb.
Example: The *committee* chooses its own chairman.

Common Noun—a noun that indicates any one of a class of persons, places, or things.
Examples: *boy; town; ball.*

Comparative Adjective—an adjective form (ending in —er or adding the word *more* before the word) used when two person or things are compared.
Example: This apple is *smaller* and *more delicious* than that one.

Complex Sentence—a sentence containing one independent clause and one or more dependent clauses.
Example: *I went to town to shop, but found that all the stores were closed.*

Compound Sentence—a sentence containing two or more independent clauses joined by a conjunction.
Example: *I called my friend, and we talked for an hour.*

Compound-Complex Sentence—a sentence that has two or more independent clauses and at least one dependent or subordinate clause.
Example: *When she opened the door, there was no one on the porch, and the street was empty, too.*

Concrete Noun—a noun that names a physical, visible, or tangible item.
Example: *airplane.*

Conjunction—a word that connects words, phrases, or clauses.
Example: I like toast *and* jam.

Coordinating Conjunction—a conjunction used to connect two independent clauses.
Example: He grinned, *and* I giggled.

Correlative Conjuction—conjunctions which are used in pairs.
Example: *Neither* Alan *nor* Amy will go.

Dependent (or Subordinate) Clause— a clause that functions as a noun, adjective, or adverb within a sentence, but cannot stand alone.
Example: *What she said* was true.

Direct Object—the noun, pronoun, or noun phrase in a sentence which receives the action of a transitive verb.
Example: I threw the *ball*.

Gerund—a verb form ending in *-ing*, usually used as a noun.
Example: *Skiing* is fun.

Indefinite Pronoun—a pronoun that does not specify the identity of its object.
Example: *Anyone* can come.

Independent Clause—a clause which contains at least a subject and a predicate, and is capable of standing alone.
Example: *I went to the store.*

Indirect Object—the noun, pronoun, or noun phrase named as the one to or for whom action involving a direct object is done.
Example: He threw *me* the ball.

Infinitive—a non-inflected verb form usually preceeded by *to,* used as a noun, adjective, or adverb.
Example: *To run* fast is fun.

Intensive Pronoun—a pronoun which is used for emphasis.
Example: I *myself* saw it.

Interjection—an exclamatory word or phrase.
Example: *Hey! Look out!*

Intransitive Verb—a verb that cannot take an object.
Example: She *learns* easily.

Linking Verb—a verb that can be followed by an adjective that modifies the subject.
Example: Randy *is* tall.

Modify—to qualify or limit the meaning of.
Example: *very* small.

Noun—a word that names a person, place, or thing.
Examples: *girl; city; hat.*

Paragraph—a distinct division within a written work that may consist of several sentences or just one, that expresses something relevant to the whole work but is complete within itself.

Passive Voice—a verb which expresses state of being and cannot take a direct object.
Example: He *was asked* to leave.

Past Tense—a verb form that expresses action or condition that occurred in the past.
Example: Yesterday I *went* to town.

Personal Pronoun—a pronoun that denotes the speaker, person spoken to, or person spoken about.
Example: *You* can find it.

Positive Adjective—an adjective form used to assign a quality to the word it modifies.
Example: the *fast* car.

Possessive Pronoun—a pronoun that shows possession.
Example: That car is *mine.*

Predicate—the portion of a sentence or clause that tells something about the subject, consisting of a verb and possibly including objects, modifiers, and/or verb complements.

Predicate Adjective—an adjective that refers to, describes, or limits the subject of a sentence.
Example: The rock is *heavy*.

Predicate Nominative—a noun following a form of the verb *to be* in a sentence which modifies the subject.
Example: She is *Alicia*.

Preposition—a word that shows relationship (often between verbs and nouns or nouns and nouns) and takes an object.
Example: Put it *on* the table.

Prepositional Phrase—a group of words in a sentence that includes a preposition and its object, along with any modifiers of the object.
Example: Put it *on the first table*.

Present Tense—a verb form that expresses current time.
Example: I *am* here.

Pronoun—a word that takes the place of a noun.
Example: *I; you; she; it; he.*

Proper Noun—a noun that names a particular person, place, or thing, and is capitalized.
Examples: *Omaha; Jenny.*

Reflexive Pronoun—a pronoun that ends in -self or -selves; used to point the action back to the subject.
Example: You will hurt *yourself*.

Relative Pronoun—a pronoun that shows a relationship.
Example: It was he *who* did it.

Run-On (or Fused) Sentence—a sentence in which two complete sentences are run together with no punctuation to separate them.
Example: *I went to the movie I ate some popcorn.*

Sentence—a basic unit of language which must contain a subject and a predicate.
Example: *I went to the movie.*

Subject—a word or phrase in a sentence that is the doer of the action, or receives the action (in passive voice), or which is described; must agree in number with the predicate.
Example: *Margaret* was there.

Subjunctive (or Conditional) Mood—a set of verb forms used to express contingent or hypothetical action, usually introduced by *if, that*, etc., and always taking the plural form of the verb.
Example: *If I were you*, I'd go.

Superlative Adjective—an adjective form (ending in —*est* or adding the word *most* before the word) used when three or more things are involved in a comparison.
Example: This is the *slowest* of all cars.

Transitive—a verb which can take an object within a sentence.
Example: He *threw* the ball.

Verb—a word that shows action, state of being, or occurrence.
Examples: *run; is; find.*

Author	Selected Works	Writing Style Specialty
Alcott, Louisa May	*Little Women* *Little Men*	Characterization
Andersen, Hans Christian	*Andersen's Fairy Tales*	Fantasy
Blume, Judith	*Are You There, God? It's Me, Margaret.* *Then Again, Maybe I Won't*	Plot and Sequence
Carroll, Lewis	*Alice's Adventures in Wonderland* *Through the Looking Glass*	Imagery
Cather, Willa	*My Antonia* *Death Comes for the Archbishop*	Characterization; Plot and Sequence
cummings, e. e.	*Tulips and Chimneys* *Poems 1923-1954*	Poetry
Dahl, Roald	*Charlie and the Chocolate Factory* *The Magic Finger*	Plot and Sequence
Dickens, Charles	*A Christmas Carol* *David Copperfield*	Simple ideas, beautifully expressed
Grimm, Jacob and Wilhelm	*Grimms' Fairy Tales*	Fantasy
Halliburton, Richard	*The Royal Road to Romance* *The Flying Carpet*	Journalism
Henry, O.	*The Four Million* *Works of O. Henry*	Short Story Mastery
Keats, Ezra Jack	*The Snowy Day* *Whistle for Willie*	Simple ideas, beautifully expressed
Kipling, Rudyard	*The Jungle Books* *Just So Stories*	Plot and Sequence
Krauss, Ruth	*A Hole Is to Dig* *A Very Special House*	Simple ideas, beautifully expressed
Lear, Edward	*The Complete Nonsense Book* *The Jumblies*	Humor
L'Engle, Madeline	*A Wrinkle in Time* *Meet the Austins*	Plot and Sequence
Longfellow, Henry W.	*Voices of the Night* *Ballads and Other Poems*	Poetry
McCloskey, Robert	*Make Way for Ducklings* *Time of Wonder*	Plot and Sequence
Milne, A. A.	*When We Were Very Young* *Now We Are Six*	Rhythm

Author	Selected Works	Writing Style Specialty
Nash, Ogden	*Good Intentions* *I'm a Stranger Here Myself*	Humor; Coined Words
Riley, James Whitcomb	*The Old Swimmin' Hole* *'Leven More Poems*	Poetry
Rossetti, Christina	*Sing Song* *Goblin Market and Other Poems*	Poetry
Sandburg, Carl	*Rootabaga Stories* *Wind Song*	Description; Figures of Speech
Sendak, Maurice	*Where the Wild Things Are* *In The Night Kitchen*	Fantasy
Seuss, Dr.	*The Cat in the Hat* *Bartholomew and the Oobleck*	Coined Words; Originality
Silverstein, Shel	*Where the Sidewalk Ends* *Lafcadio*	Divergent Thinking; Humor
Steele, William O.	*The Perilous Road* *Wayah of the Real People*	Plot and Sequence
Stevenson, Robert Louis	*A Child's Garden of Verses*	Poetry
Teasdale, Sara	*Stars Tonight* *Strange Victory*	Lovely Word Usage
Tolkien, J. R. R.	*The Hobbit* *Lord of the Rings*	Creating a believable mythical world
Twain, Mark	*The Adventures of Tom Sawyer* *The Adventures of Huckleberry Finn*	Characterization; Description
Viorst, Judith	*Alexander and the Terrible, Horrible, No Good, Very Bad Day* *Alexander, Who Use to Be Rich Last Sunday*	Brings extraordinary qualities to everyday experiences
White, E. B.	*Charlotte's Web* *The Trumpet of the Swan*	Description; Imagery
Zoloto, Charlotte	*A Father Like That* *When I Have a Son*	Simple ideas, beautifully expressed

Dictionaries

The American Heritage Dictionary of the English Language
 W. Morris, ed. American Heritage Pub. Co./Houghton Mifflin
Bernstein's Reverse Dictionary
 Bernstein. The New York Times Book Co.
The Complete Rhyming Dictionary
 C. Wood, ed. Doubleday & Co.
Doublespeak Dictionary
 W. Lambdin. Pinnacle.
Macmillan Dictionary for Children
 P. R. Winant, sup. ed. Macmillan Pub. Co., Inc.
New Rhyming Dictionary and Poet's Handbook
 Hohnson. Harper & Row.
Webster's New World Speller/Divider
 ————. W. Collins, Pub.
Webster's Seventh New Collegiate Dictionary
 ————. G. and C. Merriam Co.

Grammar and Usage

The Art of Styling Sentences
 Waddell, Esch, and Walker. Barrons.
The Complete Letter Writer
 N. H. and S. K. Mager. Simon & Schuster.
The Golden Book on Writing
 Lambuth. Penguin.
Instant Vocabulary
 Ehrlich. Pocket Books.
Letters for All Occasions
 Myers. Barnes and Noble.
The New York Times Manual of Style and Usage
 L. Jordan, ed. Quadrangle/The New York Times Book Co.
Use the Right Word
 S. I. Hayakawa, ed. The Reader's Digest Assn., Inc.
Word Watcher's Handbook
 Martin. David McKay Co., Inc.
Write It Right
 Kredenser. Barnes and Noble.
The Written Word
 A. D. Steinhardt, sup. ed. Houghton Mifflin.

Quotations and Slang

Bartlett's Familiar Quotations
 E. M. Beck, ed. Little, Brown & Co.
Dictionary of American Slang
 Wentworth and Flexner. Simon and Schuster.
The International Thesaurus of Quotations
 R. T. Tripp, comp. Thomas Y. Crowell Co.

Thesauri

A Basic Dictionary of Synonyms and Antonyms
 L. Urdang. Elsevier/Nelson Books.
The Clear and Simple Thesaurus Dictionary
 Wittels and Greisman. Grosset and Dunlap.
Roget's International Thesaurus, 3rd ed.
 ————. Thomas Y. Crowell Co.
The Word Finder
 E. J. Fluck, et al. Rodale Press.

REASONING

TABLE OF CONTENTS

SOME COMMON SENSE APPROACHES TO PROBLEM SOLVING

- Avoid prejudices based on past experiences or limited understanding of the specific problem.

- Defer judgment until you have all the facts.

- Approach the problem in a positive and confident manner.

- Look at the problem from a "futuristic" perspective to determine if the projected solution will make sense in the future.

- Consider all possible solutions before zeroing in on the best three. Begin the "consideration" process anew, and rank the best three in 1-2-3 order.

- Organize all the data related to the problem, and categorize it as to "very important," "important," and "not important" in terms of a possible solution.

- Trust your intuition, and use it as a cornerstone for developing a strategy for problem solving. Remember, however, a cornerstone is only the beginning point. Don't neglect to examine, evaluate, and plan on the basis of all the real data available.

- Be willing to devote the time, energy and personal commitment to creative problem solving.

- Internalize the problem before considering solution possibilities.

- Outline the problem and the proposed solution. Establish realistic goals, and develop a check list and time frame to use as a guide to goal fulfillment.

- Examine the projected solution in terms of your responsibilities and life style to make sure the plan is a realistic one.

- Talk the problem over with someone whose judgment and problem-solving ability you respect. State the problem as openly and objectively as possible, and solicit constructive comments and analysis, not opinionated suggestions.

- Do not entertain plans for a partial solution or a stop-gap measure. This kind of action will only force you to begin the entire problem-solving process anew at a less opportune time.

- Write down the problem and all the possible solutions. This will help you to segregate the real issues, and to evaluate more clearly the implications of each possible solution.

- Develop a back-up strategy for a proposed solution. In the event your first approach begins to falter, move to your back-up immediately and positively.

2

WHAT WOULD YOU DO?

Write one complete sentence that suggests two ways to handle each of the following situations—one proposing a poor solution, and one proposing a good solution.

1. You were being chased by an elephant.
2. You received a nasty letter from a stranger.
3. You inherited a million dollars.
4. You met a fire-eating dragon face to face.
5. You found yourself in a haunted house at midnight.
6. The principal asked you to take charge of the entire school for a day.
7. Someone handed you three double-dip ice cream cones at noon on a hot day.
8. You found yourself lost in a deep, dark forest.
9. You had to walk to school during a rain shower with no umbrella or raincoat.
10. The only food you had to eat for a week was asparagus.
11. Someone left a tiny puppy in a basket on your doorstep.
12. You were accused of a crime you didn't commit.
13. You found a wallet containing three one-hundred dollar bills on the sidewalk.
14. A fairy godmother suddenly appeared to grant one wish for you.
15. Your best friend was quarantined with a contagious disease for a month.
16. You were asked to spend a week on tour with the president of your country.
17. All the books in the world were destroyed.
18. You broke out in a rash from head to toe on the doctor's day off.
19. You had to cross a river without a bridge or a boat.
20. You met a real live leprechaun at midnight on the eve of St. Patrick's Day.
21. It rained continuously for forty days and forty nights.
22. While fishing in a pond near your home, you hooked an alligator.
23. Someone delivered sixty-nine crates of ripe tomatoes to your house.
24. A neighbor gave you a map of the neighborhood with an X marking the spot where a hidden treasure is supposedly buried.
25. You opened the kitchen door early one morning to find a huge banner proclaiming you "Citizen of the Day."
26. After a sudden rain, you followed a rainbow to its end, and found a real pot of gold with instructions to spend it all before nightfall.
27. The king of a very important country asked you to live in the palace and be his chief assistant for onr year.
28. You found yourself responsible for planning an after-school educational program for all the children under twelve in your town.
29. None of the trees in the world had names, and, without help, you had to write a book naming and describing each tree.
30. You awakened at your school desk and were told that you had been asleep for six weeks.
31. Someone gave you a magic airplane ticket with which you could travel to any place in the world. One catch: it's a one-way ticket only!
32. You are performing on a stage before thousands of people, and your trousers fall down.
33. You are making an emergency trip down a two-lane mountain road, and you find a huge boulder blocking the road.

A CHECK LIST TO ENCOURAGE CREATIVE THINKING

Try something new each week.	
Write down weekly goals, and evaluate goal achievement regularly.	
Write down one thing that bothers you, and write a proposed plan for changing it.	
Read one easy book and one hard book.	
Keep a daily journal.	
Talk to three people about a topic that interests you. Compare and contrast their opinions.	
Read a daily newspaper.	
Read two different newspaper accounts of a news event, and compare the two.	
Read an editorial from the Sunday newspaper. Question the position taken, and mentally take your own stand.	
Poll your classmates on a topic of current interest. Graph or chart the results.	
Add ten new words to your vocabulary.	
Write an original poem, story, or song. Reread it a day later, and try to make it more interesting or exciting.	
Learn something new about a city or country.	
Study the life and times of a famous person.	
Select a subject to research. Use three different sources, and summarize your findings.	
Create a new code, and share it.	
Participate in a good brainstorming session.	
Select one current event from the news, and predict what will happen in the next seven days. Write your prediction down, and check it against the actual happenings at the end of the week.	
Do a page of difficult math problems.	
Keep a sequential record of some aspect of your environment (growth of a plant; the weather, etc.). Review the record, note changes, and the causes and effects of the changes.	
Make out a creative but realistic budget for the week.	
Work a word puzzle.	
Make up a word puzzle, and ask someone to solve it.	
Evaluate your progress in school.	
Make something out of three-dimensional materials.	
Make a list of things to do next week—some practical and some just-for-fun things.	
Share an imaginative, unusual, or "way-out" idea with someone. Note the reaction.	
Make a list of three questions you'd like to find answers for in the coming week.	
Observe the behavior of someone your own age over a period of several hours. Think about the causes and consequences of the behavior.	
Experiment to find new uses for common household products.	

WORDS AND PHRASES THAT BREED AND AID IDEA PRODUCTION

illustrate	diagram	organize	extend	magnify
subtract	alter	substitute	extrude	rearrange
fallen	minimize	integrate	transpose	flatten
adapt	abstract	eliminate	unify	modify
symbolize	add	segregate	reverse	invert
rotate	translate	stretch	separate	distort
complement	elaborate	dissect	combine	squeeze
multiply	freeze	thicken	lighten	relate
increase	decrease	regulate	turn	convert
alter	shift	modulate	mold	stain
modernize	variegated	mutate	revolutionize	arrange
superimpose	recast	affirm	edit	vary
revamp	patch	adjust	impair	mar
bend	strain	twist	adulterate	dye
denature	cover	mask	disguise	shuffle
conceal	transfigure	reorder	crossbreed	process

Name as many things as possible that _____.

How many ways can you think of to _____?

What are all the meanings you can think of for _____?

How many different ways can you express _____?

List every fact you can think of related to _____.

The answer is _____. List as many questions as you can think of for which that is the answer.

What are all the words you could use instead of_____?

How many different ways can you show _____?

How would this look to a _____?

What would happen if _____?

How is _____ like _____?

How would you feel if _____?

How would this be viewed by _____?

How would someone else feel if you _____?

Think about it . . . then, give a good answer for each situation.

1. If you bit into a solid gold coin while eating a pancake in a restaurant, who would own the coin—you or the restaurant owner? Why?

2. If your brand-new flashlight exploded, causing a fire which completely destroyed a friend's bicycle parked in your neighbor's front yard, who would be legally responsible for replacing the bicycle—you, your friend, or the manufacturer of the flashlight? Why?

3. If Peter picked a peck of peppers in Paul's pepper patch; and Paul picked ½ bushel of peppers in Peter's pepper patch; and if Paula picked ½ peck of peppers in Paul's pepper patch, 1 peck of peppers in Peter's pepper patch, and 1 peck of peppers in her own pepper patch; and, if the three put all the peppers together and divided them equally, who would end up with the most peppers from someone else's patch other than his/her own—Peter, Paul, or Paula? Why?

4. If you had no pencil, no paper, and no telephone, and you absolutely had to send a message to a friend in another town, what would you do?

THINK OF TEN ORIGINAL, NEVER-BEFORE-THOUGHT-OF . . .

ways to report on a book read.
ways to serve potatoes.
titles for patriotic songs.
uses for ice cubes.
ways to say, "I love you."
recipes using chocolate.
names for romantic novels.
uses for last year's calendar.
ways to help people less fortunate
  than yourself.
games to play with three other
  people.
four-line rhymes.
words with definitions.
holidays.
subjects to study in school.
ways to honor senior citizens.
educational toys.
colors.
substitutes for shoes.
themes for amusement parks.
Halloween masks.
uses for peach pits.

WAYS TO ORGANIZE INFORMATION

Synopsize
Make a card file.
Code.
Categorize.
Diagram.
Outline.
List.
Map.
Catalog.
Schedule.
Index.
Keep a journal.
Make a table.
Create a layout
Make a sketch.
Make a file.
Serialize.
Alphabetize.
Order numerically.
Classify by theme or subject.
Order qualitatively.
Make a time line.
Order sequentially.
Make a mock-up.

Make a list of:

1. Twenty ways to move a heavy box from one room to another.
2. Fifteen uses for a potato masher (other than mashing potatoes).
3. Forty-nine four-syllable words.
4. Sixteen uses for or things to do with an old newspaper.
5. Foods from countries other than your own (list the country for each).
6. Six places in your own community where you could go to observe animals in their natural habitats.
7. The full names of sixteen people over seventy years old.
8. Ten toys that would be safe for a year-old baby to play with.
9. Five ways to put out a fire.
10. Twenty-nine minerals.
11. Fifty-two vegetables (two that begin with each letter in the alphabet).
12. Fourteen words that name something to be worn on a person's head.
13. Twenty-two well-known bodies of water.
14. Twelve ways to save money.
15. Sixteen things to write with.
16. Twelve holidays (give the date and the symbol for each).
17. Ten sources you could use to locate information on Antarctica.
18. Authors of books you have read during the past three months.
19. Forty color words.
20. Twenty uses for a lemon.
21. Twenty-four analogies.
22. Fifteen kinds of boats.
23. Fifteen things to wear on your feet.
24. Ten things that could be used to hold papers together.
25. Thirty-six musical instruments.
26. Six ways to cook tomatoes.
27. One hundred two parts of an automobile.
28. Nine ways to tell time.
29. Twenty-one careers in the world of the theater.
30. Twenty-six cities west of the Mississippi River.
31. Ten kinds of beans.
32. Eight words that mean "cold."
33. Forty-five varieties of trees.
34. Eight ways to cook without electricity.
35. Roman Numerals from one through one hundred. Then, multiply each number on your list by ten, and write the products in Roman numerals.
36. Six places where you could find the correct spellings of the continents.
37. Fifty-nine kinds of sandwiches.
38. A dozen ways to use eggshells.
39. The ten most recent chief executives of your country.
40. Seventy-seven words that begin with the letter s (without using the dictionary).
41. The full names of all the teachers you have ever had.
42. Seven different kinds of grain used to make bread.
43. The ten largest cities in the world.

BRAINSTORMING GUIDE—
A SPRINGBOARD TO DIVERGENT THINKING

WHY?

The intended result of brainstorming is to generate a large number of ideas which will lead to a larger number of creative solutions to a given problem.

Two secondary benefits are to be derived from this process:
1. Students learn to express their ideas freely, without fear of criticism.
2. Students learn to build upon each other's ideas.

HOW?

There are four requirements for a profitable brainstorming session:

1. All ideas are accepted—defer judgment and criticism.
2. Participants must feel free to say everything they think and to hold nothing back. The "farther out" the ideas are, the better.
3. Participants build on the ideas of others. (Don't wait for a new idea to come; let it grow out of the last idea given by altering that idea in some way.)
4. Strive for quantity! The more ideas, the better.

FOLLOW-UP

After the brainstorming session:

1. Leave all ideas written as they were recorded.
2. Enlist student participation in setting some standards for evaluating and pruning the collected ideas. (The criteria will depend somewhat on the ultimate goal for use of the ideas.)
   Examples: Is the idea practical?
   Can we really accomplish it?
   Is it compatible with everyday living?
   Does it solve a problem without creating a new one?
3. Discuss which ideas fit the criteria.
4. Decide on ways to develop the ideas (like making a model, diagram, design, drawing, writing descriptive material, etc.).

GAMES THAT SHARPEN LOGICAL THINKING SKILLS

BATTLESHIP by Milton Bradley
BOGGLE by Parker Brothers
CLUE by Parker Brothers
EQUATIONS by Wff 'N Proof
MASTER-MIND by Invicta Plastics
PROBE by Parker Brothers

PSYC-OUT by Mag Nif
QUBIC by Parker Brothers
STOCK MARKET by the 3M Company
TAC-TICKLE by Wff 'N Proof
TUF by Avalon Hill
WFF 'N PROOF by Wff 'N Proof

8

1. Relate each letter of the message to the letter which follows it in the alphabet.
   HELP = IFMQ

2. Relate each letter of the message to the letter preceding it in the alphabet.
   HELP = GDKO

3. Relate each letter of the message to a letter of the alphabet which is a certain interval away from the original letter (i.e.: five letters following or three letters preceding it in the alphabet).
   HELP = MJQU or EBIM

4. Relate each letter to the letter of the alphabet which is the same distance from the end of the alphabet as this letter is from the beginning (i.e.: A = Z; B = Y; C = X, etc.).
   HELP = SVOK

5. Relate each letter to the numeral that denotes its sequence in the alphabet (i.e.: A = 1; B = 2, etc.).
   HELP = 8, 5, 12, 16

6. Relate each letter to a double letter code consisting of the letter preceding it and the letter following it in the alphabet (i.e.: A = ZB; B = AC, etc.).
   HELP = GI, DF, KM, OQ

7. Relate each letter of the alphabet to a code word. (The code word may or may not begin with that letter.)
   HELP = HORSES EAT LITTLE PEOPLE.

8. Relate each letter of the alphabet to a special pictorial system (i.e.: H =⫫; E =�; L =❗; P =🌱). 
   HELP = ⫫ ⅋ ❗ 🌱

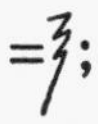

9. Use the times tables to construct a matrix; assign a letter or word to each product of the matrix. Then use the multipliers as your code.
   HELP = 4 × 1, 3 × 4, 4 × 4, 1 × 7.

10. Use a simple grid like this one:

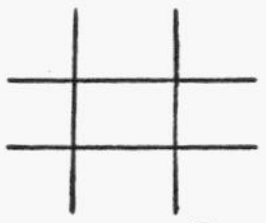

    Assign a letter or word to each section. Note that each section has a different border. Use these borders as your code.

H	O	T
B	E	P
S	A	L

    HELP = ⌐ □ ⌐ ⊏

11. Relate each letter to a color. Use colored squares or dots to write your message. (H =▨ ; E =▩ ; L =□ ; P =◩.)
    HELP = ▨▩□◩

12. Relate each letter to a part of your body. To send a message, merely point to the proper parts in sequence.

13. Relate each letter to a body movement. Then, dance your message!

14. Relate each letter to a three-dimensional item. (Each item might end with the letter it represents.) Keep these items in a code kit or box. When you are ready to send a message, spell it out with these items.
    HELP = 🎩 ✂ ✏ ♪

15. Create a flag to correlate with each letter of the alphabet. Then, use the flags to send your message.

16. Use the dot-dash International Morse Code system, and write your message.
    HELP = ...-.. .—.
17. Use the Morse Code with a flashlight or spotlight.
18. Use the Braille System as your base code. Use cardboard, styrofoam, or heavy paper and a large pin for writing your message.
    HELP = :: :: :: ::
19. Create a system of sounds—one to represent each letter or one to represent each sound in the language. Send your message in a series of sounds.
20. To send a message that self-destructs, create a taste code! Use flavors and textures of food. (You might use a different flavor lollipop for each vowel, and a different flavor cracker, cookie, or chip for each consonant.) Then, the receiver may eat the message!
21. In the same manner as #20, create a texture or shape code which can be read blindfolded by tactile means.
22. Assign the name of an animal to each letter of the alphabet (i.e.: A = Ant; B = Bat; C = Cat, etc.) Use either the name or a picture of each animal to write your message.
    HELP = HORSE; ELEPHANT; LION; PUMA
23. Arrange the letters of your message in 5- or 6-letter groups. Then, reverse the order of the letters in each group.
    Message: Leave keys in the box.
    Step #1:   leave keysi ntheb ox.
    Step #2:   evael isyek behtn xo.
24. Write your message so that only every fifth letter should be extracted to spell out the encoded message.
    HELP = trutH is ovEr all aPplied.
25. Graph your message. Predetermine a position on the graph for each letter. Then, write your message by tracing the points on the graph.

GENERAL PRINCIPLES

In order to decode a substitute cipher system, you must first try to discover how frequently any letter occurs in a given sentence.

On the average, the five vowels (a, e, i, o, u) make up 40% of the letters in the words of the English language. The letters l, n, r, s, and t make up another 30%. The least often used letters (comprising only 2%) are j, k, q, x, and z.

The letter e usually appears most frequently. The next common letters are t, a, and o. The word the is the most common three-letter word.

If you can ascertain that the first letter of a two-letter word is a t, the second letter is always o.

TO DECODE

1. Count the number of times a given symbol, number, or substitute letter appears in the coded message.

2. Those letters that appear most often should be e, t, a, and o.

3. If the same combination of three letters or symbols appears several times in the coded message, it is most probable that these letters will represent the word the. By making this assumption, and by writing the letters t, h, and e under all the corresponding letters or symbols, you will begin to see the form of several words in the message.

4. Go back and label similarly any two-letter words beginning with t by adding o.

5. Now, write o's under all the corresponding symbols.

6. Continue by conjecture with the remaining two- and three-letter words, which will eventually lead to the unlocking of most of the vowels. By this time, enough words should be partially apparent to lead to the identity of the rest of the missing letters.

+ plus
− minus
± plus or minus
∓ minus or plus
× multiplied by
÷ divided by
= equal to
≠ or ≢ not equal to
≈ or ≑ nearly equal to
≡ identical with
≢ not identical with
≎ equivalent
∼ difference
≅ congruent to
> greater than
≯ not greater than
< less than
≮ not less than
≧ or ≥ greater than or equal to
≦ or ≤ less than or equal to
| | absolute value
∪ logical sum or union
∩ logical product or intersection
⊂ is contained in
∈ is a member of; permittivity; mean error
: is to; ratio
:: as; proportion
≐ approaches
⟶ approaches limit of
∝ varies as
‖ parallel
⊥ perpendicular
∠ angle
∟ right angle
△ triangle
□ square
▭ rectangle
▱ parallelogram
○ circle
⌒ arc of circle
⟂ equilateral
≜ equiangular
√ radical; root; square root
∛ cube root
∜ fourth root
Σ sum
! or ∟ factorial product
∞ infinity
∫ integral
ƒ function
∂ or δ differential; variation
π pi
∴ therefore
∵ because
‾ vinculum (above letter)
( ) parentheses

[ ] brackets
| | braces
° degree
′ minute
″ second
△ increment
ω angular frequency; solid angle
Ω ohm
μΩ microhm
MΩ megohm
Φ magnetic flux
Ψ dielectric flux; electrostatic flux
ρ resistivity
Λ equivalent conductivity
ℛ reluctance
→ direction of flow
⇌ electric current
⬡ benzene ring
→ yields
⇌ reversible reaction
↓ precipitate
↑ gas
‰ salinity
☉ or ⊛ sun
● or ⊙ new moon
☽ first quarter
○ or ⊗ full moon
☾ last quarter
☿ Mercury
♀ Venus
♁ or ⊕ Earth
♂ Mars
♃ Jupiter
♄ Saturn
♅ Uranus
♆ Neptune
♇ Pluto
♈ Aries
♉ Taurus
♊ Gemini
♋ Cancer
♌ Leo
♍ Virgo
♎ Libra
♏ Scorpius
♐ Sagittarius
♑ Capricornus
♒ Aquarius
♓ Pisces
☌ conjunction
☍ opposition
△ trine
□ quadrature
✳ sextile
☊ dragon's head, ascending node
☋ dragon's tail, descending node

⊕ rain
✻ snow
⊠ snow on ground
← floating ice crystals
▲ hail
△ sleet
∨ frostwork
⊔ hoarfrost
≡ fog
∞ haze; dust haze
⊤ thunder
< sheet lightning
⊙ solar corona
⊕ solar halo
↰ thunderstorm
↘ direction
○ or ☉ or ⊙ annual
☉☉ or ② biennial
♃ perennial
♂ or δ male
♀ female
□ male (in charts)
○ female (in charts)
℞ take (from Latin *Recipe*)
ĀĀ or Ā or āā of each (doctor's prescription)
℔ pound
℥ ounce
ℨ dram
℈ scruple
ƒℨ fluid ounce
ƒℨ fluid dram
♍ minim
& or ℰ and; ampersand
℔ per
number
/ virgule; slash; solidus, shilling
© copyright
% per cent
℅ care of
℀ account of
@ at
∗ asterisk
† dagger
‡ double dagger
§ section
☞ index
´ acute
` grave
˜ tilde
ˆ circumflex
¯ macron
˘ breve
¨ dieresis
¸ cedilla
∧ caret

ANALOGIES

Five is to ten as eight is to sixteen.
Bake is to cake as broil is to meat.
Octopus is to ocean as tiger is to jungle.
Add is to subtract as multiply is to divide.
Sing is to voice as dance is to legs.
Ink is to pen as paint is to brush.
Brush is to comb as fork is to knife.
Milk is to cereal as bacon is to eggs.
Syrup is to pancakes as jelly is to toast.
Goose is to gander as cow is to bull.
Channel is to TV as station is to radio.
Down is to up as low is to high.
Elbow is to arm as knee is to leg.
Ankle is to foot as wrist is to hand.
Top is to bottom as back is to front.
Yellow is to a lemon as green is to celery.
Hour is to day as week is to month.
Cup is to drink as plate is to eat.
Mare is to pony as cow is to calf.
Listen is to hear as look is to see.
Bee is to hive as bird is to nest.
Gold is to mine as oil is to well.
Pie is to dessert as lettuce is to salad.
Gasoline is to car as diesel is to train.
Tomato is to fruit as corn is to vegetable.
Bus is to driver as ship is to captain.
Nail is to finger as hair is to head.
Music is to radio as program is to TV.
Automobile is to vehicle as top is to toy.

Big is to little as small is to large.
High is to low as up is to down.
Good is to bad as night is to day.
Chocolate is to vanilla as dark is to light.
Shirt is to pants as socks are to shoes.
Few is to many as some is to all.
Smoke is to fire as rain is to clouds.
On is to off as start is to stop.
Go is to green as stop is to red.
Toe is to foot as finger is to hand.
A picture is to a person as a map is to a city.
Teacher is to student as coach is to player.
Centimeter is to meter as inch is to yard.
A ship is to the sea as a plane is to the air.
Ring is to finger as watch is to arm.
Ounce is to pound as gram is to kilogram.
Second is to minute as minute is to hour.
Quart is to ounce as liter is to milliliter.
Writer is to a book as illustrator is to a picture.
Brothers is to boys as sisters is to girls.
Cut is to scissors as slice is to knife.
Water is to a plant as food is to people.
Napkin is to lap as tablecloth is to table.
Capital is to city as capitol is to building.
Candy is to sweet as lemon is to sour.
Stove is to cook as car is to ride.
Dresses are to ladies as booties are to babies.

A bed is to a bedroom as a bathtub is to a bathroom.
A den is to a fox as a nest is to a bird.
A chick is to a hen as a kitten is to a cat.
A princess is to a prince as a queen is to a king.
A lady is to a gentleman as a woman is to a man.
Eye is to see as ear is to hear.
A teacher is to a classroom as a principal is to a school.
Commercial is to TV as ad is to newspaper.
Horizontal is to the ground as vertical is to a tree.
Enter is to exit as come is to go.
Boat is to lake as ship is to ocean.
A day is to a week as a month is to a year.
A cavity is to a dentist as a mystery is to a detective.
An insect is to little as a hippopotamus is to big.
Stone is to hard as sand is to soft.
Meow is to a cat as hiss is to a snake.
A cage is to a parakeet as an aquarium is to a fish.
A bat is to a ball as a screwdriver is to a screw.
Clothes are to people as fur is to animals.
Lead is to a pencil as tobacco is to a pipe.
Hamburger is to french fries as steak is to potato.
A page is to a book as a piece is to a puzzle.
Laugh is to cry as smile is to frown.
A clock is to time as a thermometer is to temperature.
Sun is to solar energy as water power is to electricity.
Glasses are to eyes as a pacemaker is to a heart.
Air conditioning is to summer as heating is to winter.
A whale is to a minnow as an elephant is to a mouse.
Job is to work as party is to play.
Crayons are to drawing as paintbrushes are to painting.
Salt water is to ocean as fresh water is to lake.

13

WORD GAMES TO CREATE
FOR
EXERCISE IN LOGICAL THINKING

1. Use the successive letters of the alphabet as a determinate for creating a list of words having to do with any given subject. Two or more players may take turns, and the first player not able to come up with an answer loses.

    Theme: Vegetables
    Examples: A—artichoke
    B—bean
    C—corn
    etc.

2. Create an alphabetical list of words, all containing a specified letter in a specified position.

    Examples: <u>a</u> n a <u>t</u> o m y
    <u>b</u> r o <u>th</u> e r
    <u>c</u> a p <u>t</u> a i n

3. Try a contest with yourself or among several contestants to see how many words containing a specified letter sequence can be listed.

    Examples: RTH   NTR   ACH
    birth   entry   reach
    earth   sentry   each
    north   untrue   machine

4. Create word mazes on a given theme. Use twenty squares. Find words by beginning in any square and moving from letter to letter in any direction; horizontally, vertically, or diagonally, until a word is completed. No letter may be used twice in succession.

    Example: Theme: ANIMALS

L	A	W	O	H
I	R	C	G	D
S	O	N	A	I
H	E	E	P	T

Answers: dog, hog, cat,
    pig, sheep,
    horse, cow, lion

5. Create a game in which the object of the game is to discover the "rule" or criteria of the game. The player(s) may ask questions that can be answered with yes or no, but the literal meaning of the questions is of no significance.

    Example: "Rule" of the game: Only questions whose last word begins with the letter l are acceptable.
    Thus: Does it have to be living? (Answer: yes)
    Are you lying? (Answer: yes)
    Was your last response true? (Answer: no)

By continuing to ask questions, player(s) deduce the criteria by which their questions are judged and discover the "rule" of the game.

6. A word category game, such as the one that follows, forces recall, application, and synthesis.

   Form a matrix which presents any five categories across the top and any five letters down the side. The object of the game is to supply one word which satisfies both factors. The game may be played against an opponent or against time. Change categories and letters for each game.

   Example:

	Animals	Games	Vegetables	Cities	Historical Figures
S	snake	Sorry	spinach	Savannah	Stalin
P	possum	Parchesi	peas	Paducah	Patton
A					
F					
T					

7. Create a word game which fits the following format.

   Use a grid of twenty-five squares. Provide twenty-five letters. The letters must be entered in the squares so as to form 2-, 3-, 4-, and 5-letter words which will read correctly both vertically and horizontally. Each letter must be used, and may be used only once. Each word is worth five points. Two points are subtracted for each letter not used. The player who has the most points wins.
   Example: E E N O T S P A P E O T L A E N R O S T A E E N E

S	T	R	A	P
O				
A				
S				
T				

8. Fluency in association is greatly stimulated by this game. Make two lists of words. Write them opposite each other with three or four blanks between them. Fill in the blanks so that each word across will have some meaningful relationship with the word preceding it and the word following it.

   Examples:

sour	lemon	twist	dance	shoe
cloud	rain	hat	Easter	rabbit
desk				view
cat				cry
race				trip